# Cincinnati Reds 2021

## A Baseball Companion

*Edited by Steven Goldman and Bret Sayre*

Baseball Prospectus

Craig Brown, Associate Editor
Robert Au, Harry Pavlidis and Amy Pircher, Statistics Editors

Copyright © 2021 by DIY Baseball, LLC.
All rights reserved

This book or any part thereof may not be reproduced or transmitted in any form or by any means, electronic or mechanical, including photocopying, recording, or by any information storage and retrieval system, without permission in writing from the publisher.

Limit of Liability/Disclaimer of Warranty: While the publisher and the author have used their best efforts in preparing this book, they make no representations or warranties with respect to the accuracy or completeness of the contents of this book and specifically disclaim any implied warranties of merchantability or fitness for a particular purpose. No warranty may be created or extended by sales representatives or written sales materials. The advice and strategies contained herein may not be suitable for your situation. You should consult with a professional where appropriate. Neither the publisher nor the author shall be liable for any loss of profit or any other commercial damages, including but not limited to special, incidental, consequential, or other damages.

Library of Congress Cataloging-in-Publication Data:
paperback
ISBN-13: 978-1-950716-37-1

Project Credits
Cover Design: Ginny Searle
Interior Design and Production: Amy Pircher, Robert Au
Layout: Amy Pircher, Robert Au

Baseball icon courtesy of Uberux, from https://www.shareicon.net/author/uberux

Ballpark diagram courtesy of Lou Spirito/THIRTY81 Project, https://thirty81project.com/

Manufactured in the United States of America
10 9 8 7 6 5 4 3 2 1

# Table of Contents

Statistical Introduction .................................................. v

## Part 1: Team Analysis

Performance Graphs .................................................. 3

2020 Team Performance .............................................. 4

2021 Team Projections ............................................... 5

Team Personnel ..................................................... 6

Great American Ball Park Stats ...................................... 7

Reds Team Analysis ................................................. 9

## Part 2: Player Analysis

Reds Player Analysis ............................................... 16

Reds Prospects .................................................... 89

## Part 3: Featured Articles

Reds All-Time Top 10 Players ...................................... 101
    by Steven Goldman

A Taxonomy of 2020 Abnormalities ................................. 107
    by Rob Mains

Tranches of WAR .................................................. 113
    by Russell A. Carleton

Secondhand Sport ................................................. 119
    by Patrick Dubuque

Steve Dalkowski Dreaming .......................................... 123
    by Steven Goldman

A Reward For A Functioning Society ................................ 127
    by Cory Frontin and Craig Goldstein

Index of Names .................................................... 131

# Statistical Introduction

Sports are, fundamentally, a blend of athletic endeavor and storytelling. Baseball, like any other sport, tells its stories in so many ways: in the arc of a game from the stands or a season from the box scores, in photos, or even in numbers. At Baseball Prospectus, we understand that statistics don't replace observation or any of baseball's stories, but complement everything else that makes the game so much fun.

What stats help us with is with patterns and precision, variance and value. This book can help you learn things you may not see from watching a game or hundred, whether it's the path of a career over time or the breadth of the entire MLB. We'd also never ask you to choose between our numbers and the experience of viewing a game from the cheap seats or the comfort of your home; our publication combines running the numbers with observations and wisdom from some of the brightest minds we can find. But if you *do* want to learn more about the numbers beyond what's on the backs of player jerseys, let us help explain.

## Offense

We've revised our methodology for determining batting value. Long-time readers of the book will notice that we've retired True Average in favor of a new metric: Deserved Runs Created Plus (DRC+). Developed by Jonathan Judge and our stats team, this statistic measures everything a player does at the plate–reaching base, hitting for power, making outs, and moving runners over–and puts it on a scale where 100 equals league-average performance. A DRC+ of 150 is terrific, a DRC+ of 100 is average and a DRC+ of 75 means you better be an excellent defender.

DRC+ also does a better job than any of our previous metrics in taking contextual factors into account. The model adjusts for how the park affects performance, but also for things like the talent of the opposing pitcher, value of different types of batted-ball events, league, temperature and other factors. It's able to describe a player's expected offensive contribution than any other statistic we've found over the years, and also does a better job of predicting future performance as well.

The other aspect of run-scoring is baserunning, which we quantify using Baserunning Runs. BRR not only records the value of stolen bases (or getting caught in the act), but also accounts for all the stuff that doesn't show up on the back of a baseball card: a runner's ability to go first to third on a single, or advance on a fly ball.

## Defense

Where offensive value is *relatively* easy to identify and understand, defensive value is … not. Over the past dozen years, the sabermetric community has focused mostly on stats based on zone data: a real-live human person records the type of batted ball and estimated landing location, and models are created that give expected outs. From there, you can compare fielders' actual outs to those expected ones. Simple, right?

Unfortunately, zone data has two major issues. First, zone data is recorded by commercial data providers who keep the raw data private unless you pay for it. (All the statistics we build in this book and on our website use public data as inputs.) That hurts our ability to test assumptions or duplicate results. Second, over the years it has become apparent that there's quite a bit of "noise" in zone-based fielding analysis. Sometimes the conclusions drawn from zone data don't hold up to scrutiny, and sometimes the different data provided by different providers don't look anything alike, giving wildly different results. Sometimes the hard-working professional stringers or scorers might unknowingly inflict unconscious bias into the mix: for example good fielders will often be credited with more expected outs despite the data, and ballparks with high press boxes tend to score more line drives than ones with a lower press box.

Enter our Fielding Runs Above Average (FRAA). For most positions, FRAA is built from play-by-play data, which allows us to avoid the subjectivity found in many other fielding metrics. The idea is this: count how many fielding plays are made by a given player and compare that to expected plays for an average fielder at their position (based on pitcher ground ball tendencies and batter handedness). Then we adjust for park and base-out situations.

When it comes to catchers, our methodology is a little different thanks to the laundry list of responsibilities they're tasked with beyond just, well, catching and throwing the ball. By now you've probably heard about "framing" or the art of making umpires more likely to call balls outside the strike zone for strikes. To put this into one tidy number, we incorporate pitch tracking data (for the years it exists) and adjust for important factors like pitcher, umpire, batter and home-field advantage using a mixed-model approach. This grants us a number for how many strikes the catcher is personally adding to (or subtracting from) his pitchers' performance … which we then convert to runs added or lost using linear weights.

Framing is one of the biggest parts of determining catcher value, but we also take into account blocking balls from going past, whether a scorer deems it a passed ball or a wild pitch. We use a similar approach—one that really benefits from the pitch tracking data that tells us what ends up in the dirt and what doesn't. We also include a catcher's ability to prevent stolen bases and how well they field balls in play, and *finally* we come up with our FRAA for catchers.

## Pitching

Both pitching and fielding make up the half of baseball that isn't run scoring: run prevention. Separating pitching from fielding is a tough task, and most recent pitching analysis has branched off from Voros McCracken's famous (and controversial) statement, "There is little if any difference among major-league pitchers in their ability to prevent hits on balls hit in the field of play." The research of the analytic community has validated this to some extent, and there are a host of "defense-independent" pitching measures that have been developed to try and extract the effect of the defense behind a hurler from the pitcher's work.

Our solution to this quandary is Deserved Run Average (DRA), our core pitching metric. DRA seeks to evaluate a pitcher's performance, much like earned run average (ERA), the tried-and-true pitching stat you've seen on every baseball broadcast or box score from the past century, but it's very different. To start, DRA takes an event-by-event look at what the pitchers does, and adjusts the value of that event based on different environmental factors like park, batter, catcher, umpire, base-out situation, run differential, inning, defense, home field advantage, pitcher role and temperature. That mixed model gives us a pitcher's expected contribution, similar to what we do for our DRC+ model for hitters and FRAA model for catchers. (Oh, and we also consider the pitcher's effect on basestealing and on balls getting past the catcher.)

DRA is set to the scale of runs allowed per nine innings (RA9) instead of ERA, which makes DRA's scale slightly higher than ERA's. Because of this, for ease of use, we're supplying DRA-, which is much easier for the reader to parse. As with DRC+, DRA- is an "index" stat, meaning instead of using some arbitrary and shifting number to denote what's "good," average is always 100. The reason that it uses a minus rather than a plus is because like ERA, a lower number is better. Therefore a 75 DRA- describes a performance 25 percent better than average, whereas a 150 DRA- means that either a pitcher is getting extremely lucky with their results, or getting ready to try a new pitch.

Since the last time you picked up an edition of this book, we've also made a few minor changes to DRA to make it better. Recent research into "tunneling"—the act of throwing consecutive pitches that appear similar from a batter's point of view until after the swing decision point–data has given us a new contextual factor to account for in DRA: plate distance. This refers to the distance between successive pitches as they approach the plate, and while it has a smaller effect than factors like velocity or whiff rate, it still can help explain pitcher strikeout rate in our model.

## Recently Added Descriptive Statistics

Returning to our 2021 edition of the book are a few figures which recently appeared. These numbers may be a little bit more familiar to those of you who have spent some time investigating baseball statistics.

### Fastball Percentage

Our fastball percentage (FA%) statistic measures how frequently a pitcher throws a pitch classified as a "fastball," measured as a percentage of overall pitches thrown. We qualify three types of fastballs:

1. The traditional four-seam fastball;
2. The two-seam fastball or sinker;
3. "Hard cutters," which are pitches that have the movement profile of a cut fastball and are used as the pitcher's primary offering or in place of a more traditional fastball.

For example, a pitcher with a FA% of 67 throws any combination of these three pitches about two-thirds of the time.

### Whiff Rate

Everybody loves a swing and a miss, and whiff rate (Whiff%) measures how frequently pitchers induce a swinging strike. To calculate Whiff%, we add up all the pitches thrown that ended with a swinging strike, then divide that number by a pitcher's total pitches thrown. Most often, high whiff rates correlate with high strikeout rates (and overall effective pitcher performance).

### Called Strike Probability

Called Strike Probability (CSP) is a number that represents the likelihood that all of a pitcher's pitches will be called a strike while controlling for location, pitcher and batter handedness, umpire and count. Here's how it works: on each pitch, our model determines how many times (out of 100) that a similar pitch was called for a strike given those factors mentioned above, and when normalized for each batter's strike zone. Then we average the CSP for all pitches thrown by a pitcher in a season, and that gives us the yearly CSP percentage you see in the stats boxes.

As you might imagine, pitchers with a higher CSP are more likely to work in the zone, where pitchers with a lower CSP are likely locating their pitches outside the normal strike zone, for better or for worse.

## Projections

Many of you aren't turning to this book just for a look at what a player has done, but for a look at what a player is going to do: the PECOTA projections. PECOTA, initially developed by Nate Silver (who has moved on to greater fame as a political analyst), consists of three parts:

1. Major-league equivalencies, which use minor-league statistics to project how a player will perform in the major leagues;
2. Baseline forecasts, which use weighted averages and regression to the mean to estimate a player's current true talent level; and
3. Aging curves, which uses the career paths of comparable players to estimate how a player's statistics are likely to change over time.

With all those important things covered, let's take a look at what's in the book this year.

## Team Prospectus

Most of this book is composed of team chapters, with one for each of the 30 major-league franchises. On the first page of each chapter, you'll see a box that contains some of the key statistics for each team as well as a very inviting stadium diagram.

We start with the team name, their unadjusted 2020 win-loss record, and their divisional ranking. Beneath that are a host of other team statistics. **Pythag** presents an adjusted 2020 winning percentage, calculated by taking runs scored per game (**RS/G**) and runs allowed per game (**RA/G**) for the team, and running them through a version of Bill James' Pythagorean formula that was refined and improved by David Smyth and Brandon Heipp. (The formula is called "Pythagenpat," which is equally fun to type and to say.)

Next up is **DRC+**, described earlier, to indicate the overall hitting ability of the team either above or below league-average. Run prevention on the pitching side is covered by **DRA** (also mentioned earlier) and another metric: Fielding Independent Pitching (**FIP**), which calculates another ERA-like statistic based on strikeouts, walks, and home runs recorded. Defensive Efficiency Rating (**DER**) tells us the percentage of balls in play turned into outs for the team, and is a quick fielding shorthand that rounds out run prevention.

After that, we have several measures related to roster composition, as opposed to on-field performance. **B-Age** and **P-Age** tell us the average age of a team's batters and pitchers, respectively. **Payroll** is the combined team payroll for all on-field players, and Doug Pappas' Marginal Dollars per Marginal Win (**M$/MW**) tells us how much money a team spent to earn production above replacement level.

Next to each of these stats, we've listed each team's MLB rank in that category from first to 30th. In this, first always indicates a positive outcome and 30th a negative outcome, except in the case of salary—first is highest.

After the franchise statistics, we share a few items about the team's home ballpark. There's the aforementioned diagram of the park's dimensions (including distances to the outfield wall), a graphic showing the height of the wall from the left-field pole to the right-field pole, and a table showing three-year park factors for the stadium. The park factors are displayed as indexes where 100 is average, 110 means that the park inflates the statistic in question by 10 percent, and 90 means that the park deflates the statistic in question by 10 percent.

On the second page of each team chapter, you'll find three graphs. The first is **Payroll History** and helps you see how the team's payroll has compared to the MLB and divisional average payrolls over time. Payroll figures are current as of January 1, 2021; with so many free agents still unsigned as of this writing, the final 2021 figure will likely be significantly different for many teams. (In the meantime, you can always find the most current data at Baseball Prospectus' Cot's Baseball Contracts page.)

The second graph is **Future Commitments** and helps you see the team's future outlays, if any.

The third graph is **Farm System Ranking** and displays how the Baseball Prospectus prospect team has ranked the organization's farm system since 2007.

After the graphs, we have a **Personnel** section that lists many of the important decision-makers and upper-level field and operations staff members for the franchise, as well as any former Baseball Prospectus staff members who are currently part of the organization. (In very rare circumstances, someone might be on both lists!)

## Position Players

After all that information and a thoughtful bylined essay covering each team, we present our player comments. These are also bylined, but due to frequent franchise shifts during the offseason, our bylines are more a rough guide than a perfect accounting of who wrote what.

Each player is listed with the major-league team that employed him as of early January 2021. If a player changed teams after that point via free agency, trade, or any other method, you'll be able to find them in the chapter for their previous squad.

As an example, take a look at the player comment for Padres shortstop Fernando Tatis Jr.: the stat block that accompanies his written comment is at the top of this page. First we cover biographical information (age is as of June 30, 2021) before moving onto the stats themselves. Our statistic columns include standard identifying information like **YEAR**, **TEAM**, **LVL** (level of affiliated play) and **AGE** before getting into the numbers. Next, we provide raw, untranslated

www.baseballprospectus.com

## Fernando Tatis Jr.  SS
Born: 01/02/99   Age: 22   Bats: R   Throws: R
Height: 6'3"   Weight: 217   Origin: International Free Agent, 2015

| YEAR | TEAM | LVL | AGE | PA | R | 2B | 3B | HR | RBI | BB | K | SB | CS | AVG/OBP/SLG |
|---|---|---|---|---|---|---|---|---|---|---|---|---|---|---|
| 2018 | SA | AA | 19 | 394 | 77 | 22 | 4 | 16 | 43 | 33 | 109 | 16 | 5 | .286/.355/.507 |
| 2019 | SD | MLB | 20 | 372 | 61 | 13 | 6 | 22 | 53 | 30 | 110 | 16 | 6 | .317/.379/.590 |
| 2020 | SD | MLB | 21 | 257 | 50 | 11 | 2 | 17 | 45 | 27 | 61 | 11 | 3 | .277/.366/.571 |
| 2021 FS | SD | MLB | 22 | 600 | 95 | 24 | 4 | 31 | 81 | 50 | 165 | 17 | 8 | .263/.331/.499 |
| 2021 DC | SD | MLB | 22 | 628 | 100 | 25 | 4 | 32 | 85 | 53 | 173 | 19 | 8 | .263/.331/.499 |

Comparables: Darryl Strawberry, Bo Bichette, Ronald Acuña Jr.

| YEAR | TEAM | LVL | AGE | PA | DRC+ | BABIP | BRR | FRAA | WARP |
|---|---|---|---|---|---|---|---|---|---|
| 2018 | SA | AA | 19 | 394 | 136 | .370 | 3.0 | SS(83): -1.9 | 2.4 |
| 2019 | SD | MLB | 20 | 372 | 118 | .410 | 7.1 | SS(83): 0.9 | 3.4 |
| 2020 | SD | MLB | 21 | 257 | 126 | .306 | 0.7 | SS(57): -5.5 | 0.9 |
| 2021 FS | SD | MLB | 22 | 600 | 126 | .318 | 1.7 | SS -1 | 3.9 |
| 2021 DC | SD | MLB | 22 | 628 | 126 | .318 | 1.8 | SS -1 | 4.0 |

numbers like you might find on the back of your dad's baseball cards: **PA** (plate appearances), **R** (runs), **2B** (doubles), **3B** (triples), **HR** (home runs), **RBI** (runs batted in), **BB** (walks), **K** (strikeouts), **SB** (stolen bases) and **CS** (caught stealing).

Following the basic stats is **Whiff%** (whiff rate), which denotes how often, when a batter swings, he fails to make contact with the ball. Another way to think of this number is an inverse of a hitter's contact rate.

Next, we have unadjusted "slash" statistics: **AVG** (batting average), **OBP** (on-base percentage) and **SLG** (slugging percentage). Following the slash line is **DRC+** (Deserved Runs Created Plus), which we described earlier as total offensive expected contribution compared to the league average.

**BABIP** (batting average on balls in play) tells us how often a ball in play fell for a hit, and can help us identify whether a batter may have been lucky or not ... but note that high BABIPs also tend to follow the great hitters of our time, as well as speedy singles hitters who put the ball on the ground.

The next item is **BRR** (Baserunning Runs), which covers all of a player's baserunning accomplishments including (but not limited to) swiped bags and failed attempts. Next is **FRAA** (Fielding Runs Above Average), which also includes the number of games previously played at each position noted in parentheses. Multi-position players have only their two most frequent positions listed here, but their total FRAA number reflects all positions played.

Our last column here is **WARP** (Wins Above Replacement Player). WARP estimates the total value of a player, which means for hitters it takes into account hitting runs above average (calculated using the DRC+ model), BRR and FRAA. Then, it makes an adjustment for positions played and gives the player a credit

# Cincinnati Reds 2021

for plate appearances based upon the difference between "replacement level"—which is derived from the quality of players added to a team's roster after the start of the season–and the league average.

The final line just below the stats box is **PECOTA** data, which is discussed further in a following section.

## Catchers

Catchers are a special breed, and thus they have earned their own separate box which displays some of the defensive metrics that we've built just for them. As an example, let's check out Yasmani Grandal.

| YEAR | TEAM | P. COUNT | FRM RUNS | BLK RUNS | THRW RUNS | TOT RUNS |
|---|---|---|---|---|---|---|
| 2018 | LAD | 16816 | 15.7 | 0.8 | 0.1 | 16.5 |
| 2019 | MIL | 18740 | 19.4 | 1.8 | -0.1 | 21.1 |
| 2020 | CHW | 4830 | 3.7 | 0.3 | -0.2 | 3.8 |
| 2021 | CHW | 14430 | 16.7 | -0.6 | 1.0 | 17.1 |
| 2021 | CHW | 14430 | 16.7 | 0.4 | 1.0 | 18.0 |

The **YEAR** and **TEAM** columns match what you'd find in the other stat box. **P. COUNT** indicates the number of pitches thrown while the catcher was behind the plate, including swinging strikes, fouls and balls in play. **FRM RUNS** is the total run value the catcher provided (or cost) his team by influencing the umpire to call strikes where other catchers did not. **BLK RUNS** expresses the total run value above or below average for the catcher's ability to prevent wild pitches and passed balls. **THRW RUNS** is calculated using a similar model as the previous two statistics, and it measures a catcher's ability to throw out basestealers but also to dissuade them from testing his arm in the first place. It takes into account factors like the pitcher (including his delivery and pickoff move) and baserunner (who could be as fast as Billy Hamilton or as slow as Yonder Alonso). **TOT RUNS** is the sum of all of the previous three statistics.

## Pitchers

Let's give our pitchers a turn, using 2020 AL Cy Young winner Shane Bieber as our example. Take a look at his stat block: the first line and the **YEAR**, **TEAM**, **LVL** and **AGE** columns are the same as in the position player example earlier.

Here too, we have a series of columns that display raw, unadjusted statistics compiled by the pitcher over the course of a season: **W** (wins), **L** (losses), **SV** (saves), **G** (games pitched), **GS** (games started), **IP** (innings pitched), **H** (hits allowed) and **HR** (home runs allowed). Next we have two statistics that are rates: **BB/9** (walks per nine innings) and **K/9** (strikeouts per nine innings), before returning to the unadjusted K (strikeouts).

xii - Statistical Introduction

Next up is **GB%** (ground ball percentage), which is the percentage of all batted balls that were hit on the ground, including both outs and hits. Remember, this is based on observational data and subject to human error, so please approach this with a healthy dose of skepticism.

**BABIP** (batting average on balls in play) is calculated using the same methodology as it is for position players, but it often tells us more about a pitcher than it does a hitter. With pitchers, a high BABIP is often due to poor defense or bad luck, and can often be an indicator of potential rebound, and a low BABIP may be cause to expect performance regression. (A typical league-average BABIP is close to .290-.300.)

The metrics **WHIP** (walks plus hits per inning pitched) and **ERA** (earned run average) are old standbys: WHIP measures walks and hits allowed on a per-inning basis, while ERA measures earned runs on a nine-inning basis. Neither of these stats are translated or adjusted.

**DRA-** (Deserved Run Average) was described at length earlier, and measures how the pitcher "deserved" to perform compared to other pitchers. Please note that since we lack all the data points that would make for a "real" DRA for minor-league events, the DRA- displayed for minor league partial-seasons is based off of different data. (That data is a modified version of our cFIP metric, which you can find more information about on our website.)

## Shane Bieber   RHP

Born: 05/31/95   Age: 26   Bats: R   Throws: R
Height: 6'3"   Weight: 200   Origin: Round 4, 2016 Draft (#122 overall)

| YEAR | TEAM | LVL | AGE | W | L | SV | G | GS | IP | H | HR | BB/9 | K/9 | K | GB% | BABIP |
|---|---|---|---|---|---|---|---|---|---|---|---|---|---|---|---|---|
| 2018 | AKR | AA | 23 | 3 | 0 | 0 | 5 | 5 | 31 | 26 | 1 | 0.3 | 8.7 | 30 | 47.3% | .278 |
| 2018 | COL | AAA | 23 | 3 | 1 | 0 | 8 | 8 | 48$^2$ | 30 | 3 | 1.1 | 8.7 | 47 | 52.0% | .227 |
| 2018 | CLE | MLB | 23 | 11 | 5 | 0 | 20 | 19 | 114$^2$ | 130 | 13 | 1.8 | 9.3 | 118 | 46.2% | .356 |
| 2019 | CLE | MLB | 24 | 15 | 8 | 0 | 34 | 33 | 214$^1$ | 186 | 31 | 1.7 | 10.9 | 259 | 44.4% | .298 |
| 2020 | CLE | MLB | 25 | 8 | 1 | 0 | 12 | 12 | 77$^1$ | 46 | 7 | 2.4 | 14.2 | 122 | 48.4% | .267 |
| 2021 FS | CLE | MLB | 26 | 10 | 6 | 0 | 26 | 26 | 150 | 121 | 18 | 2.1 | 11.7 | 195 | 45.5% | .297 |
| 2021 DC | CLE | MLB | 26 | 14 | 7 | 0 | 30 | 30 | 196.7 | 159 | 24 | 2.1 | 11.7 | 257 | 45.5% | .297 |

Comparables: Luis Severino, Danny Salazar, Joe Musgrove

| YEAR | TEAM | LVL | AGE | WHIP | ERA | DRA- | WARP | MPH | FB% | WHF | CSP |
|---|---|---|---|---|---|---|---|---|---|---|---|
| 2018 | AKR | AA | 23 | 0.87 | 1.16 | 61 | 0.9 | | | | |
| 2018 | COL | AAA | 23 | 0.74 | 1.66 | 69 | 1.2 | | | | |
| 2018 | CLE | MLB | 23 | 1.33 | 4.55 | 74 | 2.6 | 94.7 | 57.4% | 26.2% | |
| 2019 | CLE | MLB | 24 | 1.05 | 3.28 | 75 | 4.9 | 94.4 | 45.8% | 30.8% | |
| 2020 | CLE | MLB | 25 | 0.87 | 1.63 | 53 | 2.6 | 95.3 | 53.6% | 40.7% | |
| 2021 FS | CLE | MLB | 26 | 1.04 | 2.44 | 64 | 4.4 | 94.7 | 50.0% | 33.2% | 44.2% |
| 2021 DC | CLE | MLB | 26 | 1.04 | 2.44 | 64 | 5.8 | 94.7 | 50.0% | 33.2% | 44.2% |

Just like with hitters, **WARP** (Wins Above Replacement Player) is a total value metric that puts pitchers of all stripes on the same scale as position players. We use DRA as the primary input for our calculation of WARP. You might notice that relief pitchers (due to their limited innings) may have a lower WARP than you were expecting or than you might see in other WARP-like metrics. WARP does not take leverage into account, just the actions a pitcher performs and the expected value of those actions ... which ends up judging high-leverage relief pitchers differently than you might imagine given their prestige and market value.

**MPH** gives you the pitcher's 95th percentile velocity for the noted season, in order to give you an idea of what the *peak* fastball velocity a pitcher possesses. Since this comes from our pitch-tracking data, it is not publicly available for minor-league pitchers.

Finally, we display the three new pitching metrics we described earlier. **FB%** (fastball percentage) gives you the percentage of fastballs thrown out of all pitches. **WHF** (whiff rate) tells you the percentage of swinging strikes induced out of all pitches. **CSP** (called strike probability) expresses the likelihood of all pitches thrown to result in a called strike, after controlling for factors like handedness, umpire, pitch type, count and location.

## PECOTA

All players have PECOTA projections for 2021, as well as a set of other numbers that describe the performance of comparable players according to PECOTA. All projections for 2021 are for the player at the date we went to press in early January and are projected into the league and park context as indicated by the team abbreviation. (Note that players at very low levels of the minors are too unpredictable to assess using these numbers.) All PECOTA projected statistics represent a player's projected major-league performance.

How we're doing that is a little different this season. There are really two different values that go into the final stat line that you see for PECOTA: How a player performs, and how much playing time he'll be given to perform it. In the past we've estimated playing time based on each team's roster and depth charts, and we'll continue to do that. These projections are denoted as **2021 DC**.

But in many cases, a player won't be projected for major-league playing time; most of the time this is because they aren't projected to be major-league players at all, but still developing as prospects. Or perhaps a player will provide Triple-A depth, only to have an opportunity open up because of injury. For these purposes, we're also supplying a second projection, labeled **2021 FS**, or full season. This is what we would project the player to provide in 600 plate appearances or 150 innings pitched.

Below the projections are the player's three highest-scoring comparable players as determined by PECOTA. All comparables represent a snapshot of how the listed player was performing at the same age as the current player, so if a

23-year-old pitcher is compared to Bartolo Colón, he's actually being compared to a 23-year-old Colón, not the version that pitched for the Rangers in 2018, nor to Colón's career as a whole.

A few points about pitcher projections. First, we aren't yet projecting peak velocity, so that column will be blank in the PECOTA lines. Second, projecting DRA is trickier than evaluating past performance, because it is unclear how deserving each pitcher will be of his anticipated outcomes. However, we know that another DRA-related statistic–contextual FIP or cFIP-estimates future run scoring very well. So for PECOTA, the projected DRA- figures you see are based on the past cFIPs generated by the pitcher and comparable players over time, along with the other factors described above.

If you're familiar with PECOTA, then you'll have noticed that the projection system often appears bullish on players coming off a bad year and bearish on players coming off a good year. (This is because the system weights several previous seasons, not just the most recent one.) In addition, we publish the 50th percentile projections for each player–which is smack in the middle of the range of projected production—which tends to mean PECOTA stat lines don't often have extreme results like 40 home runs or 250 strikeouts in a given season. In essence, PECOTA doesn't project very many extreme seasons.

## Managers

After all those wonderful team chapters, we've got statistics for each big-league manager, all of whom are organized by alphabetical order. Here you'll find a block including an extraordinary amount of information collected from each manager's entire career. For more information on the acronyms and what they mean, please visit the Glossary at www.baseballprospectus.com.

There is one important metric that we'd like to call attention to, and you'll find it next to each manager's name: **wRM+** (weighted reliever management plus). Developed by Rob Arthur and Rian Watt, wRM+ investigates how good a manager is at using their best relievers during the moments of highest leverage, using both our proprietary DRA metric as well as Leverage Index. wRM+ is scaled to a league average of 100, and a wRM+ of 105 indicates that relievers were used approximately five percent "better" than average. On the other hand, a wRM+ of 95 would tell us the team used its relievers five percent "worse" than the average team.

While wRM+ does not have an extremely strong correlation with a manager, it is statistically significant; this means that a manager is not *entirely* responsible for a team's wRM+, but does have some effect on that number.

# Part 1: Team Analysis

# Performance Graphs

### *Payroll History (in millions)*

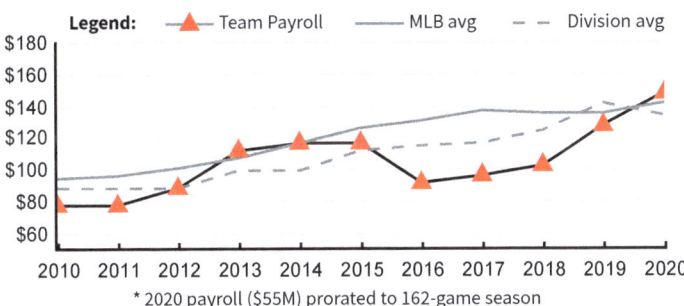

* 2020 payroll ($55M) prorated to 162-game season

### *Future Commitments (in millions)*

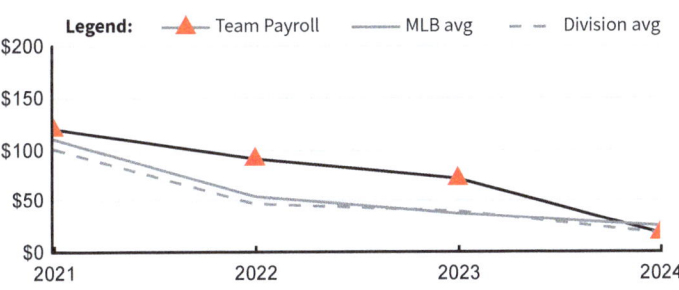

### *Farm System Ranking*

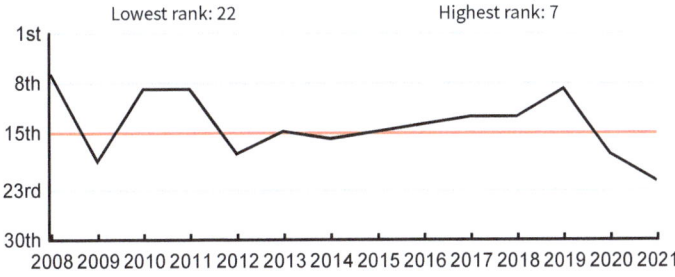

# 2020 Team Performance

## ACTUAL STANDINGS

| Team | W | L | Pct |
|---|---|---|---|
| CHC | 34 | 26 | 0.567 |
| **CIN** | **31** | **29** | **0.517** |
| STL | 30 | 28 | 0.517 |
| MIL | 29 | 31 | 0.483 |
| PIT | 19 | 41 | 0.317 |

## dWIN% STANDINGS

| Team | W | L | Pct |
|---|---|---|---|
| **CIN** | **32** | **28** | **0.537** |
| MIL | 29 | 31 | 0.496 |
| CHC | 27 | 33 | 0.465 |
| STL | 26 | 34 | 0.436 |
| PIT | 20 | 40 | 0.344 |

## TOP HITTERS

| Player | WARP |
|---|---|
| Joey Votto | 1.2 |
| Jesse Winker | 1.1 |
| Eugenio Suárez | 0.5 |

## TOP PITCHERS

| Player | WARP |
|---|---|
| Luis Castillo | 2.2 |
| Trevor Bauer | 1.4 |
| Sonny Gray | 1.3 |

## VITAL STATISTICS

| Statistic Name | Value | Rank |
|---|---|---|
| Pythagenpat | .500 | 14th |
| dWin% | .537 | 7th |
| Runs Scored per Game | 4.05 | 28th |
| Runs Allowed per Game | 4.05 | 9th |
| Deserved Runs Created Plus | 102 | 14th |
| Deserved Run Average Minus | 84 | 3rd |
| Fielding Independent Pitching | 3.94 | 5th |
| Defensive Efficiency Rating | .702 | 16th |
| Batter Age | 29.8 | 24th |
| Pitcher Age | 29.0 | 16th |
| Payroll | $55.0M | 16th |
| Marginal $ per Marginal Win | $2.9M | 13th |

# 2021 Team Projections

## PROJECTED STANDINGS

| Team | W | L | Pct | +/- |
|---|---|---|---|---|
| MIL | 89.1 | 72.9 | 0.550 | 10 |
| Adding Kolten Wong doesn't quite make this an above-average lineup, but it improves their run prevention. Playoff hopes hinge on Christian Yelich being himself again. | | | | |
| CHC | 84.9 | 77.1 | 0.524 | -6 |
| Change, though painful, will give them an overdue chance to evaluate new options. | | | | |
| STL | 80.4 | 81.6 | 0.496 | 0 |
| Nolan Arenado makes them favorites in the NL Central, but real parity with the goliaths on the coasts is still a ways off. | | | | |
| **CIN** | **79.3** | **82.7** | **0.490** | **-4** |
| Traded or non-tendered several key role players to save money, and their Cy Young winner left as a free agent. | | | | |
| PIT | 59.5 | 102.5 | 0.367 | 8 |
| This year will be about sorting out shortstop, hoping for progress from Mitch Keller, and enjoying Ke'Bryan Hayes--but not much more. | | | | |

## TOP PROJECTED HITTERS

| Player | WARP |
|---|---|
| Joey Votto | 2.8 |
| Eugenio Suárez | 2.8 |
| Nick Castellanos | 2.2 |

## TOP PROJECTED PITCHERS

| Player | WARP |
|---|---|
| Luis Castillo | 3.9 |
| Sonny Gray | 2.8 |
| Tyler Mahle | 1.8 |

## FARM SYSTEM REPORT

| Top Prospect | Number of Top 101 Prospects |
|---|---|
| Nick Lodolo, #57 | 1 |

## KEY DEDUCTIONS

| Player | WARP |
|---|---|
| Trevor Bauer | 3.4 |
| Anthony DeSclafani | 1.2 |
| Raisel Iglesias | 1.0 |
| Freddy Galvis | 0.7 |
| Curt Casali | 0.6 |
| Archie Bradley | 0.5 |

## KEY ADDITIONS

| Player | WARP |
|---|---|
| Sean Doolittle | 0.9 |

# Team Personnel

**Vice President & General Manager**
Nick Krall

**Vice President, Assistant General Manager**
Sam Grossman

**Vice President, Player Personnel**
Chris Buckley

**Vice President, Player Development**
Shawn Pender

**Manager**
David Bell

# Great American Ball Park Stats

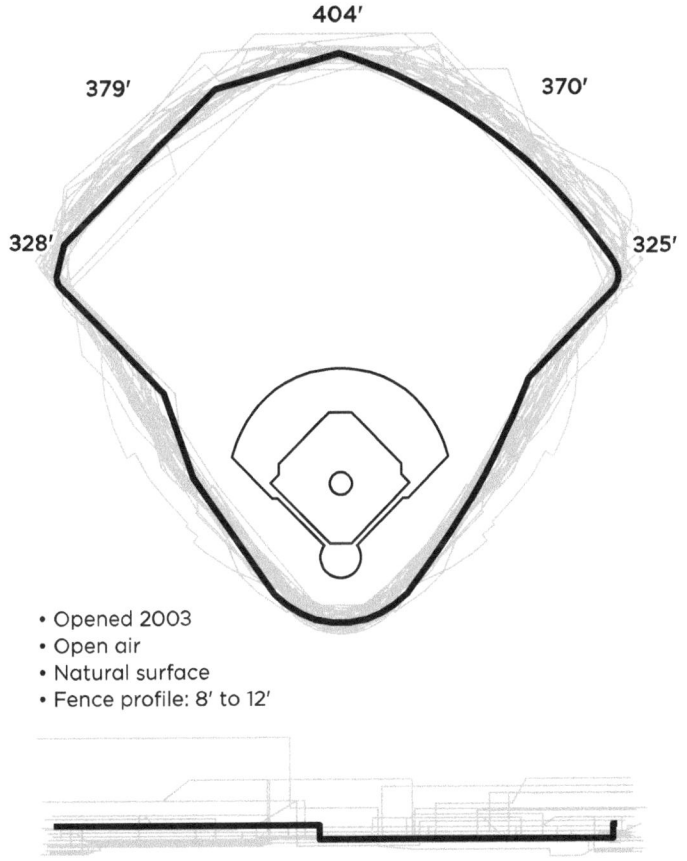

- Opened 2003
- Open air
- Natural surface
- Fence profile: 8' to 12'

## Three-Year Park Factors

| Runs | Runs/RH | Runs/LH | HR/RH | HR/LH |
|---|---|---|---|---|
| 102 | 101 | 104 | 110 | 109 |

# Reds Team Analysis

There's a moment early in Joe Morgan's career with the Reds, in many ways a forgotten one, that I turned to when learning of the Hall of Fame second baseman's death, at age 77, last fall. It is 1972 and he is in Oakland—his hometown—part of a Cincinnati team that had reached the World Series for the second time in three seasons. Morgan was meant as the last piece for a team desperate to win and win now. And yet he is still hitless going into the last of the ninth in Game Five.

But now, none of that matters. Facing elimination, the Reds have rallied and hold a one-run lead in the ninth with one out and Blue Moon Odom on third base. When Bert Campaneris hits a pop-up into foul territory, Morgan waves off first baseman Tony Perez to make the catch.

Within seconds, chaos. Stumbling after the catch, Morgan's become aware of Odom's decision to come home. He either regains his composure or has composure enough to throw to an upright Johnny Bench, who turns towards third base, tagging Odom before falling on top of him for the final out.

This is the definitive Morgan: The awareness of Odom. The ability to place the ball in the precise spot needed even after he's slipped. An understanding of where the game's greatest catcher needed it in order to make the play. A display of on-field intelligence that, even now, has few peers.

This is also Morgan's true star-turning moment. Only a year before most had never heard of him, and those within baseball viewed him as angry and underachieving, an undersized and overall pedestrian second baseman, destined to languish with the Astros. But he had been spectacular in his 1972 regular season with the Reds, and with this play he's shown that he not only belongs on this great team, but that he's determined to make it better.

"You guys didn't win anything until I got here," Morgan would say later of his time with the Reds. "You didn't save me. I saved you."

For a man who in retirement openly loathed modern metrics, there is little doubt of how well these numbers serve his legacy now. In four of his first five seasons with the Reds, his lowest WARP total was 7.7. In winning his first National League MVP Award in 1975, he had 9.5 WARP, a number Mike Trout has eclipsed only once. The following year, in earning his second MVP, he led the league not only in OBP, OPS and OPS+, but slugging as well. Even at 5-foot-7, surrounded by some of the great power hitters of their generation, Morgan showed there was nothing "little" about him.

# Cincinnati Reds 2021

There are those still in Cincinnati who will admit to how upset and even angry they were upon hearing about Morgan's arrival in a multi-player trade in the winter of 1971. It wasn't about him. Nor was it about the others the Reds would receive from Houston— including future Gold Glove center fielder César Gerónimo and pitcher Jack Billingham, who proved himself an invaluable member of the team's starting staff.

This was about the players that the Reds had sent off in return. They had handed the Astros the affable, power hitting first baseman Lee May, who, along with Perez, Johnny Bench and Pete Rose, had come through the Cincinnati system. Gone too was the former NL Rookie of the Year Tommy Helms, himself a Gold Glove second baseman. *Cincinnati Enquirer* columnist Bob Hertz equated trading these two to the United States sending "Dwight Eisenhower to the Germans during World War II." In the immediate aftermath, there were few fans who disagreed.

"We made the deal to get the balance we think we need to make us a contender," general manager Bob Howsam explained, citing Morgan's speed. "We feel we have enough power to win. May had his greatest year last year and we still finished fourth."

It all feels familiar. Howsam had seen a team that he felt that lacked diversity in its offense and felt bold, desperate measures were needed in order to make sure it returned to championship form. Now, nearly four decades later, Cincinnati finds itself in much the same place—looking back at the previous season in disbelief, trying to determine what kind of team they want to be.

"The way we built our team this year, we knew we were...probably going to be more of a power team, more station-to-station," former president of baseball operations Dick Williams told *The Athletic* after the season's disheartening end. "We don't have a lot of sprinters on this team. There's not a lot of base stealing, hit-and-run type action you're going to see. But we definitely will have the coaching staff looking, re-evaluating their messaging to the players, their approach to the players."

Williams manages to somehow temper an undeniable frustration. There is no doubt that he must have felt what so many fans did on those tortured summer afternoons and evenings for most of the "60-game sprint." By my own estimate, I watched 50 of these—what else was on?— during which I had resigned myself from the first inning on to the idea that the offense would not support the brilliant starting pitching. I was ready to watch nine innings of batters struggling to put the ball in play.

Seldom can you quantify a lack of joy. But one can here. The Reds' .212 batting average was last in the league in 2020. It also was the worst in this team's history. They ranked 28th in both doubles and runs per game. In 21 games of the abbreviated season, Cincinnati failed to score more than two runs. In his own season post-mortem, the *Enquirer's* Bobby Nightengale pointed out that the

Reds' league-worst .245 BIBP was "the lowest by any team since the 1968 New York Yankees (.241) and the second-lowest number by a team since the end of the Deadball era in 1920."

The fact they even managed to post a winning, playoff-worthy record in 2020 should have meant something. But for most of the year it did not. The team's dependence on home runs began to wear on those who waited patiently for the season, almost from the start. In theory, scoring this way should be fun. But I cannot count how times I received a message from one of the friends with whom I've shared a daily game text chain for close to a decade that proclaimed in one way or another: "A double!" Or, "A hit! An actual base hit!"

I suppose that's why the two-game collapse, a historic one, to the Braves in the Wild Card round, did not induce the same kind of anguish one might expect. You knew this, or something like this, might happen. When the Reds failed to score in the first inning of Game One when it all seemed set up for them, one felt they had returned to their August form. At that moment, going scoreless for 22 innings didn't seem implausible.

In the weeks that followed, no one I know asked "What might have been?" By this time, some were in fact ready to see the season end, move on from the very thing they felt might deliver some happiness, even when that feeling has been at a premium. The Reds simply weren't fun—even when they did win. That too feels strange to say, but only one team had a higher three-true-outcome (TTO) percentage than Cincinnati's .407, and their inability to put multiple hits together proved maddening. (Though it must be said that the only team who bested that average was the American League Champion Tampa Bay Rays, and they correctly believe that, save falling in six games in the World Series, it worked out pretty well.)

"We hit home runs, we took walks, those were great," said Reds general manager Nick Krall in one interview after being tapped to run the Baseball Operations Department following Williams' departure in the offseason. "But at the end of the day, we need to figure out how to get more singles and more runs in from the bases.

"I know that we struggled with batting average of balls in play," he went on. "We struggled with batting average in general. We've got to figure out ways to put guys in a better position to succeed or be able to have guys use the whole field and take advantage of when a shift is out there."

This struggle seemed inexplicable given the moves the team made in winter. Even with the shortened season, the Reds knew what they had in Luis Castillo, Sonny Gray and Trevor Bauer—three pitchers each of whom in any given year might be the ace on anyone's staff. They knew where to devote the large chunk of the $164 million in their free-agent money: To established hitters like Mike

# Cincinnati Reds 2021

Moustakas and Nick Castellanos, and the slight, slashing outfielder Shogo Akiyama, the Reds' first Japanese-born player. They gave this team, in the eyes of many, an actual chance to win the National League pennant.

But it didn't work, or maybe there was no way it could. The truncated season meant there was little room for error for players to work themselves out of this. Moreover, the Reds are not alone in their winter of self-reflection which, more and more, feels like an all-consuming angst. Across baseball there is an inward search going on, one that goes well beyond TTO. No less than the one-time boy prince, Theo Epstein, expressed his own concerns about what he saw, even as he made his own, hopefully temporary, exit from the game. A truncated season that so many people had waited for gave us a glimpse into baseball's troubling present. I don't think Reds fans were alone in their exasperation watching something we looked forward to, thought we needed, only to come away asking, "Did we really need *this*?"

Since the abrupt end to the campaign, few have taken solace in good things they did see: the return to winning baseball and the postseason after a seven-year absence. The late-season run in which the Reds, once left for dead, won 11 of their last 14 games to earn a spot and have a chance in October. Trevor Bauer doing what Tom Seaver and Mario Soto and Jim Maloney could not: win the National League Cy Young Award, the very first for the Reds. Akiyama's outfield play earning him consideration for a Gold Glove, and catcher Tucker Barnhart actually winning one.

Morgan, clearly sick, said nothing of the Reds troubles this summer. But, given his past comments, we know what he must have felt. In the hours of his death, after looking back at that play and thinking of what his time in Cincinnati meant to the Reds and to baseball, I realized that Morgan meant something else for many. There are those who knew him as only the sound of Sunday Night Baseball, broadcasting alongside Jon Miller on ESPN for 21 seasons.

It is not an entirely pleasant association. His commentary, especially during his last decade on the air, made Morgan the avatar of the baseball establishment, one unable to accept innovation, gripping to the past in a sport whose great failings had been an inability to act and accept change, even when it was clear that change was desperately needed.

In spite of this, there is something to gain from this part of Morgan's life. The very thing he feared has taken place in baseball and certainly with his Reds. Within his imperfect reasoning about strategy and his general on-air crankiness, one can see that certain concerns are now widespread: the precipitous decline of African-American players, predominance of the base-to-base play whose dullness threatens to keep fans away and a general disdain for creating runs through the hit-and-run and the stolen base. TTO might guarantee outcomes, but it often ensures unwatchable baseball.

There are those that have felt that with Morgan's death, it might be time to let go of the "Machine." For so long, its dominance has unfairly overshadowed every Reds team since. I've often joked that growing up in Southwest Ohio, you learn the names of the "Great Eight," the starting lineup for the team's 1975 and 1976 teams, before you're able to spell. We are reminded of them through statues around the stadium, and through the great mural that dominates the entrance to Great American Ballpark. There is a strong, smart case for finally moving on.

But they still have lessons to give. Once, Bob Howsam defied orthodoxy in making the trade with Houston, knowing that the Reds desperately needed to find a new way to win. To do this now would require a far harder reinvention, one that goes against the new precepts of baseball, one that attempts to reconcile the game's past and present.

Perhaps it's impossible. But you truly cannot honor that team, or Joe Morgan, by pining for something that you may never find again. To try, however, is perhaps the only actual path for the Reds to return to the World Series after 30 years. And to do so will require Reds ownership to demonstrate the kind of awareness that Joe Morgan displayed when he found that ball in foul territory and cocked his arm to throw, knowing a runner was breaking for home.

—*Sridhar Pappu is the author of The Year of The Pitcher: Bob Gibson, Denny McLain and the End of Baseball's Golden Age.*

# Part 2: Player Analysis

# PLAYER COMMENTS WITH GRAPHS

## Shogo Akiyama  CF
Born: 04/16/88  Age: 33  Bats: L  Throws: R
Height: 6'0"  Weight: 190  Origin: International Free Agent, 2019

| YEAR | TEAM | LVL | AGE | PA | R | 2B | 3B | HR | RBI | BB | K | SB | CS | AVG/OBP/SLG |
|---|---|---|---|---|---|---|---|---|---|---|---|---|---|---|
| 2020 | CIN | MLB | 32 | 183 | 16 | 6 | 1 | 0 | 9 | 25 | 34 | 7 | 3 | .245/.357/.297 |
| 2021 FS | CIN | MLB | 33 | 600 | 77 | 25 | 2 | 8 | 53 | 68 | 124 | | | .237/.333/.339 |
| 2021 DC | CIN | MLB | 33 | 498 | 64 | 21 | 1 | 6 | 44 | 56 | 102 | | | .237/.333/.339 |

The Akiyama that Reds fans were treated to last September is the version they hope to see going forward. You know, the lefty spark plug at the top of the order with the .317/.456/.365 batting line and five stolen bases, not the guy who slapped .196/.282/.250 up to that point. Akiyama impressed everyone out of the gate with his speed, baseball IQ and Gold Glove-caliber outfield defense, but it took a while for his offensive game to click. His power missed its flight from Japan and he struggled in limited exposure to same-side pitching, but Akiyama's tremendous contact skills and patient, all-fields approach give him a good chance to reach base at a steady clip. Even if he remains little more than a slap hitter, his combination of speed, defense and table-setting skills should make him a solid outfield contributor this year.

| YEAR | TEAM | LVL | AGE | PA | DRC+ | BABIP | BRR | FRAA | WARP |
|---|---|---|---|---|---|---|---|---|---|
| 2020 | CIN | MLB | 32 | 183 | 84 | .314 | 0.6 | LF(36): 1.2, CF(21): 1.4 | 0.5 |
| 2021 FS | CIN | MLB | 33 | 600 | 87 | .297 | | LF 4, CF 6 | 1.7 |
| 2021 DC | CIN | MLB | 33 | 498 | 87 | .297 | | LF 3, CF 5 | 1.4 |

*Shogo Akiyama, continued*

## Batted Ball Distribution

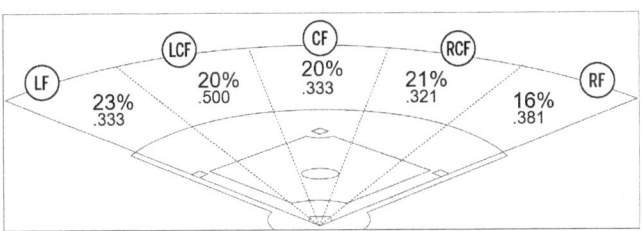

## Strike Zone vs LHP        Strike Zone vs RHP

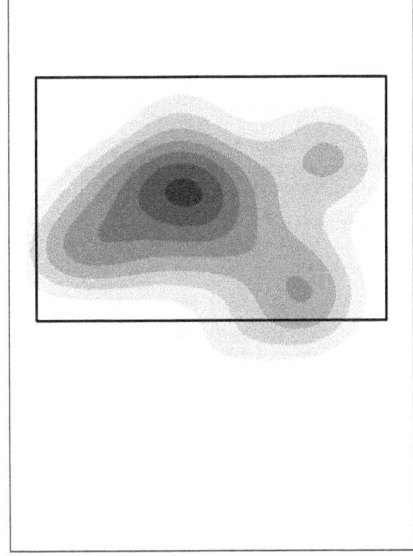

# Cincinnati Reds 2021

## Aristides Aquino  RF
Born: 04/22/94  Age: 27  Bats: R  Throws: R
Height: 6'4"  Weight: 220  Origin: International Free Agent, 2011

| YEAR | TEAM | LVL | AGE | PA | R | 2B | 3B | HR | RBI | BB | K | SB | CS | AVG/OBP/SLG |
|---|---|---|---|---|---|---|---|---|---|---|---|---|---|---|
| 2018 | PNS | AA | 24 | 445 | 49 | 20 | 2 | 20 | 55 | 35 | 112 | 4 | 5 | .240/.306/.448 |
| 2018 | CIN | MLB | 24 | 1 | 0 | 0 | 0 | 0 | 0 | 0 | 1 | 0 | 0 | .000/.000/.000 |
| 2019 | LOU | AAA | 25 | 323 | 56 | 13 | 1 | 28 | 53 | 23 | 81 | 5 | 1 | .299/.356/.636 |
| 2019 | CIN | MLB | 25 | 225 | 31 | 8 | 0 | 19 | 47 | 16 | 60 | 7 | 0 | .259/.316/.576 |
| 2020 | CIN | MLB | 26 | 56 | 7 | 1 | 0 | 2 | 8 | 6 | 18 | 1 | 0 | .170/.304/.319 |
| 2021 FS | CIN | MLB | 27 | 600 | 79 | 22 | 3 | 37 | 88 | 41 | 186 | 3 | 2 | .236/.300/.492 |
| 2021 DC | CIN | MLB | 27 | 273 | 36 | 10 | 1 | 17 | 40 | 19 | 84 | 1 | 1 | .236/.300/.492 |

Comparables: Bubba Trammell, Lyle Mouton, Jay Buhner

Despite his power-packed 2019 debut, Aquino was a victim of Cincinnati's "win now" approach last year when the signings of Nick Castellanos and Shogo Akiyama left him without a clear path to big league playing time. The recipe had called for Aquino to simmer a bit in Triple-A, but COVID-19 changed everything and he never found his power groove while shuttling in and out of the Cincinnati clubhouse. Aquino is older than you think and is a liability with the glove, but the thunder in his bat is real. Of course, so is his penchant to swing from the heels and make too little contact and too many outs, making it likely his career will take an alpine path with a few high peaks surrounding long, sustained valleys.

| YEAR | TEAM | LVL | AGE | PA | DRC+ | BABIP | BRR | FRAA | WARP |
|---|---|---|---|---|---|---|---|---|---|
| 2018 | PNS | AA | 24 | 445 | 103 | .282 | -1.3 | RF(108): 7.7 | 0.8 |
| 2018 | CIN | MLB | 24 | 1 | 87 |  | -0.7 | RF(1): -0.1 | -0.1 |
| 2019 | LOU | AAA | 25 | 323 | 148 | .321 | 0.2 | RF(64): 3.4, CF(5): 1.8 | 2.9 |
| 2019 | CIN | MLB | 25 | 225 | 114 | .266 | 0.3 | RF(54): 0.9 | 1.0 |
| 2020 | CIN | MLB | 26 | 56 | 76 | .222 | 0.3 | LF(13): 0.5, RF(4): -0.0, CF(1): -0.1 | 0.0 |
| 2021 FS | CIN | MLB | 27 | 600 | 105 | .285 | 0.1 | LF 2, RF 1 | 2.0 |
| 2021 DC | CIN | MLB | 27 | 273 | 105 | .285 | 0.0 | LF 1, RF 0 | 0.9 |

*Aristides Aquino, continued*

## Batted Ball Distribution

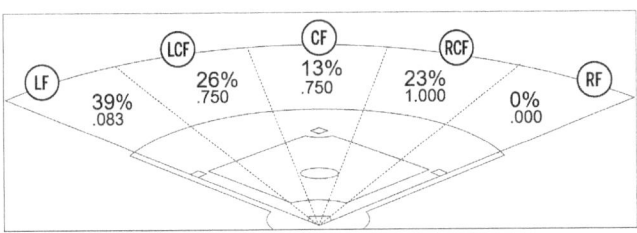

## Strike Zone vs LHP

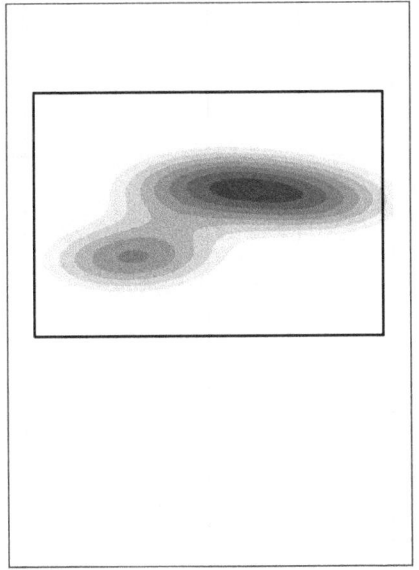

## Strike Zone vs RHP

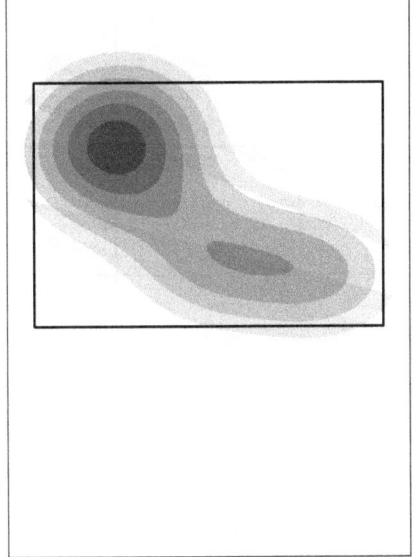

# Cincinnati Reds 2021

## Nick Castellanos  RF
Born: 03/04/92   Age: 29   Bats: R   Throws: R
Height: 6'4"   Weight: 203   Origin: Round 1, 2010 Draft (#44 overall)

| YEAR | TEAM | LVL | AGE | PA | R | 2B | 3B | HR | RBI | BB | K | SB | CS | AVG/OBP/SLG |
|---|---|---|---|---|---|---|---|---|---|---|---|---|---|---|
| 2018 | DET | MLB | 26 | 678 | 88 | 46 | 5 | 23 | 89 | 49 | 151 | 2 | 1 | .298/.354/.500 |
| 2019 | DET | MLB | 27 | 439 | 57 | 37 | 3 | 11 | 37 | 31 | 96 | 2 | 1 | .273/.328/.462 |
| 2019 | CHC | MLB | 27 | 225 | 43 | 21 | 0 | 16 | 36 | 10 | 47 | 0 | 1 | .321/.356/.646 |
| 2020 | CIN | MLB | 28 | 242 | 37 | 11 | 2 | 14 | 34 | 19 | 69 | 0 | 2 | .225/.298/.486 |
| 2021 FS | CIN | MLB | 29 | 600 | 86 | 28 | 3 | 28 | 85 | 44 | 164 | 2 | 2 | .250/.312/.472 |
| 2021 DC | CIN | MLB | 29 | 616 | 89 | 29 | 3 | 29 | 88 | 45 | 168 | 2 | 2 | .250/.312/.472 |

Comparables: Matt Williams, Todd Frazier, Travis Fryman

Most big-dollar baseball contracts are chock-full of various potential award bonuses, and some of them are fun to ponder. One example: Castellanos will take home a cool hundred large for each and every Gold Glove award he earns. Makes you wonder if he's been playing the long game as he butchers his way down the defensive spectrum, secretly taking grounders in darkened ballparks while his agent yells "Pickin' Machine!" to prepare for his shocking reveal as a premiere first sacker. Probably not; by all accounts Castellanos has worked hard to improve as an outfielder, to little avail. Luckily he can still hit the snot out of the ball, at least when he makes contact. His whiff rate spiked last year, which caused his batting average and on-base percentage to plummet. The Reds had best hope that was an anomaly rather than a trend or Castellanos is in danger of turning into an expensive out-maker instead of a middle-of-the-order force.

| YEAR | TEAM | LVL | AGE | PA | DRC+ | BABIP | BRR | FRAA | WARP |
|---|---|---|---|---|---|---|---|---|---|
| 2018 | DET | MLB | 26 | 678 | 124 | .361 | 3.4 | RF(142): -2.8 | 3.5 |
| 2019 | DET | MLB | 27 | 439 | 104 | .332 | -1.7 | RF(89): 0.9 | 1.1 |
| 2019 | CHC | MLB | 27 | 225 | 141 | .347 | 0.1 | RF(48): 0.9, LF(11): -0.6 | 1.8 |
| 2020 | CIN | MLB | 28 | 242 | 108 | .257 | -1.7 | RF(57): -3.0 | 0.2 |
| 2021 FS | CIN | MLB | 29 | 600 | 107 | .305 | -0.3 | RF 4, LF 0 | 2.1 |
| 2021 DC | CIN | MLB | 29 | 616 | 107 | .305 | -0.3 | RF 4 | 2.2 |

**Nick Castellanos, continued**

## Batted Ball Distribution

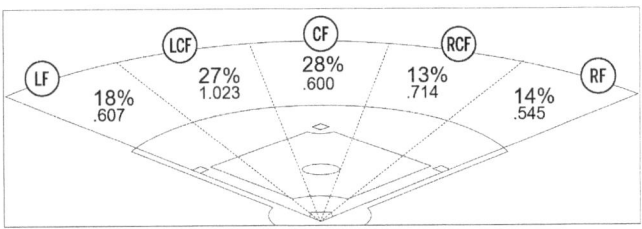

## Strike Zone vs LHP

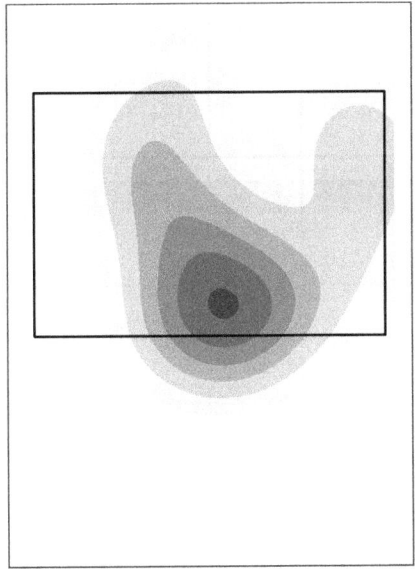

## Strike Zone vs RHP

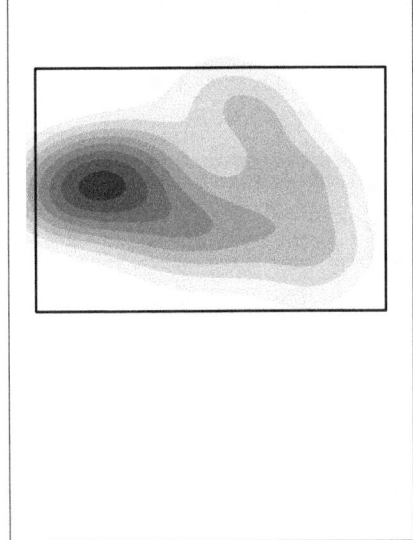

# Cincinnati Reds 2021

## Kyle Farmer  2B

Born: 08/17/90   Age: 30   Bats: R   Throws: R
Height: 6'0"   Weight: 205   Origin: Round 8, 2013 Draft (#244 overall)

| YEAR | TEAM | LVL | AGE | PA | R | 2B | 3B | HR | RBI | BB | K | SB | CS | AVG/OBP/SLG |
|---|---|---|---|---|---|---|---|---|---|---|---|---|---|---|
| 2018 | OKC | AAA | 27 | 312 | 37 | 24 | 1 | 7 | 36 | 17 | 50 | 1 | 1 | .288/.333/.451 |
| 2018 | LAD | MLB | 27 | 77 | 1 | 4 | 1 | 0 | 9 | 5 | 15 | 0 | 0 | .235/.312/.324 |
| 2019 | CIN | MLB | 28 | 197 | 22 | 6 | 0 | 9 | 27 | 10 | 59 | 4 | 1 | .230/.279/.410 |
| 2020 | CIN | MLB | 29 | 70 | 4 | 3 | 0 | 0 | 4 | 5 | 13 | 1 | 0 | .266/.329/.312 |
| 2021 FS | CIN | MLB | 30 | 600 | 67 | 24 | 1 | 18 | 68 | 37 | 140 | 1 | 1 | .234/.293/.386 |
| 2021 DC | CIN | MLB | 30 | 219 | 24 | 8 | 0 | 6 | 24 | 13 | 51 | 0 | 1 | .234/.293/.386 |

Comparables: Steve Scarsone, Danny Espinosa, Jason Maxwell

The more challenging the defensive position a backup can credibly play, the less pressure there is on his bat to earn his paycheck. By proving last year that he can handle shortstop in addition to being an actual by-gosh catcher, Farmer may have earned himself a lifetime pass to the training table even if his lumber continues to slumber. Managers will love Farmer because his peerless flexibility backstops any managerial move they can imagine making; regulars will gain comfort from the fact he's already fulfilled his career ambitions and isn't gunning for their job, unlike some 22-year-old middle infielder with invisibly quick hands and a penchant for loud contact. Farmer has enough skill with the bat to someday post a .700 OPS, but that's now become a bonus, not a requirement.

| YEAR | TEAM | LVL | AGE | PA | DRC+ | BABIP | BRR | FRAA | WARP |
|---|---|---|---|---|---|---|---|---|---|
| 2018 | OKC | AAA | 27 | 312 | 105 | .325 | -2.2 | 3B(31): 3.2, C(29): -6.9, SS(8): -0.9 | 0.3 |
| 2018 | LAD | MLB | 27 | 77 | 80 | .296 | -0.4 | 3B(22): 1.2, C(1): 0.0, 1B(1): -0.0 | 0.2 |
| 2019 | CIN | MLB | 28 | 197 | 76 | .284 | -1.5 | 2B(41): -1.0, 1B(18): -0.1, C(15): 0.2 | -0.2 |
| 2020 | CIN | MLB | 29 | 70 | 94 | .333 | -0.4 | SS(15): -0.2, 2B(13): 0.1, 3B(2): -0.1 | 0.1 |
| 2021 FS | CIN | MLB | 30 | 600 | 83 | .281 | -0.7 | SS -2, 2B -2 | 0.0 |
| 2021 DC | CIN | MLB | 30 | 219 | 83 | .281 | -0.2 | SS -1, 2B -1 | 0.1 |

**Kyle Farmer**, continued

## Batted Ball Distribution

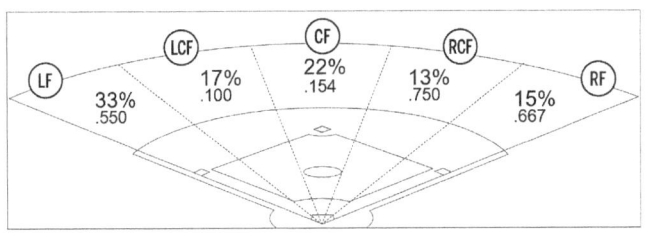

**Strike Zone vs LHP**    **Strike Zone vs RHP**

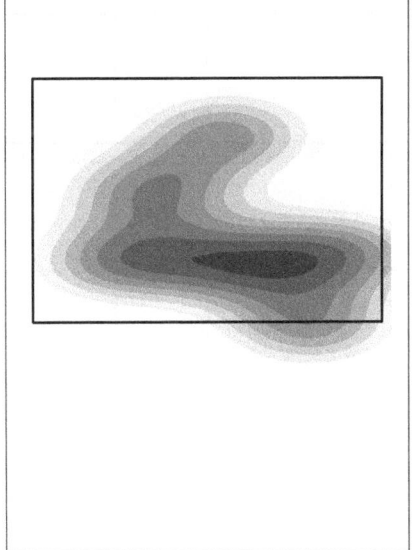

## Jose Garcia  SS

Born: 04/05/98   Age: 23   Bats: R   Throws: R
Height: 6'2"   Weight: 175   Origin: International Free Agent, 2017

| YEAR | TEAM | LVL | AGE | PA | R | 2B | 3B | HR | RBI | BB | K | SB | CS | AVG/OBP/SLG |
|---|---|---|---|---|---|---|---|---|---|---|---|---|---|---|
| 2018 | DAY | LO-A | 20 | 517 | 61 | 22 | 4 | 6 | 53 | 19 | 112 | 13 | 9 | .245/.290/.344 |
| 2019 | DAY | HI-A | 21 | 452 | 58 | 37 | 1 | 8 | 55 | 25 | 83 | 15 | 2 | .280/.343/.436 |
| 2020 | CIN | MLB | 22 | 68 | 4 | 0 | 0 | 0 | 2 | 1 | 26 | 1 | 1 | .194/.206/.194 |
| 2021 FS | CIN | MLB | 23 | 600 | 59 | 22 | 2 | 12 | 57 | 32 | 191 | 6 | 4 | .204/.260/.322 |
| 2021 DC | CIN | MLB | 23 | 311 | 30 | 11 | 1 | 6 | 29 | 16 | 99 | 3 | 2 | .204/.260/.322 |

Comparables: Chris Nelson, Marcus Semien, Gleyber Torres

Don't make too much out of Garcia's struggles at the plate last year, as the young Cuban had never before faced Double-A pitching, let alone the ungodly breaking stuff they throw in The Show. Tall and lean, Garcia's speed and natural athleticism stands out even in the lofty company of a major-league clubhouse and he impressed the brass during spring training with his high baseball IQ. At the plate he's a work in progress, with fringy power but notable bat-to-ball skills and a mature approach that give him a chance to avoid the bottom of the order. Garcia displayed a flair for the dramatic in his big-league debut and has the range and arm to be a plus shortstop. He would obviously benefit from a more normal development path, but it's easy to picture Garcia growing into a solid first-division player.

| YEAR | TEAM | LVL | AGE | PA | DRC+ | BABIP | BRR | FRAA | WARP |
|---|---|---|---|---|---|---|---|---|---|
| 2018 | DAY | LO-A | 20 | 517 | 84 | .307 | 1.8 | SS(93): -0.7, 2B(29): -1.8 | 0.3 |
| 2019 | DAY | HI-A | 21 | 452 | 143 | .329 | -0.8 | SS(100): 0.7 | 3.8 |
| 2020 | CIN | MLB | 22 | 68 | 45 | .317 | -0.8 | SS(21): 1.3 | -0.2 |
| 2021 FS | CIN | MLB | 23 | 600 | 59 | .285 | 0.2 | SS 1, 2B 0 | -1.2 |
| 2021 DC | CIN | MLB | 23 | 311 | 59 | .285 | 0.1 | SS 1 | -0.6 |

*Jose Garcia, continued*

## Batted Ball Distribution

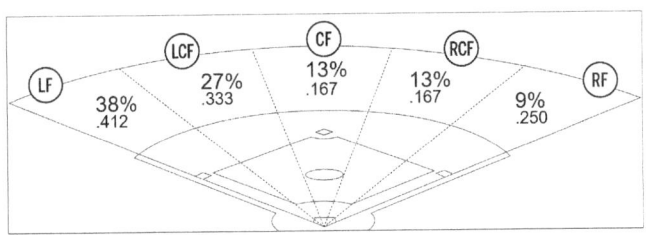

### Strike Zone vs LHP

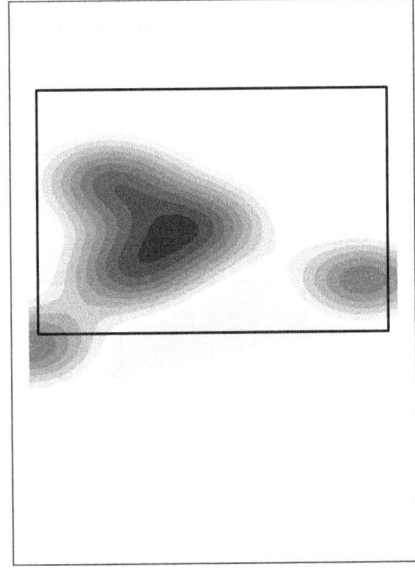

### Strike Zone vs RHP

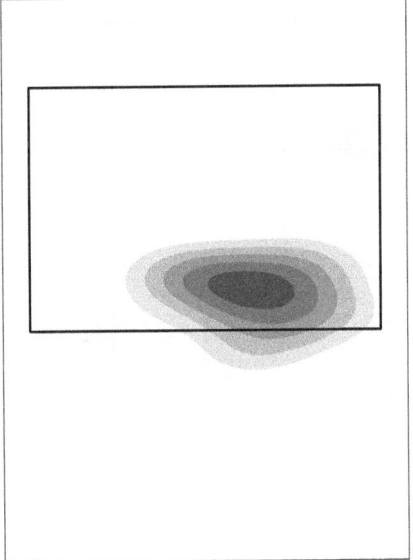

# Cincinnati Reds 2021

## Scott Heineman   RF
Born: 12/04/92   Age: 28   Bats: R   Throws: R
Height: 6'1"   Weight: 220   Origin: Round 11, 2015 Draft (#318 overall)

| YEAR | TEAM | LVL | AGE | PA | R | 2B | 3B | HR | RBI | BB | K | SB | CS | AVG/OBP/SLG |
|---|---|---|---|---|---|---|---|---|---|---|---|---|---|---|
| 2018 | FRI | AA | 25 | 31 | 6 | 2 | 0 | 1 | 10 | 7 | 5 | 2 | 1 | .522/.613/.739 |
| 2018 | RR | AAA | 25 | 469 | 68 | 20 | 2 | 11 | 57 | 32 | 93 | 16 | 8 | .295/.355/.429 |
| 2019 | NAS | AAA | 26 | 182 | 34 | 6 | 2 | 8 | 25 | 17 | 45 | 4 | 3 | .340/.412/.553 |
| 2019 | TEX | MLB | 26 | 85 | 8 | 6 | 0 | 2 | 7 | 9 | 20 | 1 | 2 | .213/.306/.373 |
| 2020 | TEX | MLB | 27 | 54 | 6 | 3 | 0 | 1 | 7 | 2 | 11 | 3 | 0 | .154/.185/.269 |
| 2021 FS | CIN | MLB | 28 | 600 | 71 | 23 | 3 | 20 | 69 | 45 | 158 | 7 | 5 | .243/.313/.408 |
| 2021 DC | CIN | MLB | 28 | 124 | 14 | 4 | 0 | 4 | 14 | 9 | 32 | 1 | 1 | .243/.313/.408 |

Comparables: Alfredo Marte, Jeff Baker, Brandon Moss

Heineman barely missed out on the family batting title this season, falling just short of his brother Tyler, a backup catcher with the Giants who hit .190. He did homer, though, whereas Tyler failed to leave the yard. One can imagine a good-natured but spirited Thanksgiving conflict over this, followed by an hour-long scoreless game of cornhole.

| YEAR | TEAM | LVL | AGE | PA | DRC+ | BABIP | BRR | FRAA | WARP |
|---|---|---|---|---|---|---|---|---|---|
| 2018 | FRI | AA | 25 | 31 | 260 | .611 | -0.9 | CF(5): -0.9, LF(2): 0.0 | 0.4 |
| 2018 | RR | AAA | 25 | 469 | 111 | .353 | 4.0 | RF(48): 1.7, CF(44): -3.3, LF(13): -0.7 | 1.4 |
| 2019 | NAS | AAA | 26 | 182 | 139 | .426 | -1.1 | RF(13): 0.8, LF(11): 1.6, 1B(9): -1.0 | 1.3 |
| 2019 | TEX | MLB | 26 | 85 | 87 | .264 | -0.5 | CF(9): -0.5, RF(8): -0.5, LF(6): 0.1 | -0.1 |
| 2020 | TEX | MLB | 27 | 54 | 81 | .175 | 0.1 | CF(17): 2.0, LF(3): -0.2, 1B(1): 0.1 | 0.2 |
| 2021 FS | CIN | MLB | 28 | 600 | 94 | .306 | 0.3 | LF 1, RF 1 | 1.2 |
| 2021 DC | CIN | MLB | 28 | 124 | 94 | .306 | 0.1 | LF 0, RF 0 | 0.2 |

*Scott Heineman, continued*

## Batted Ball Distribution

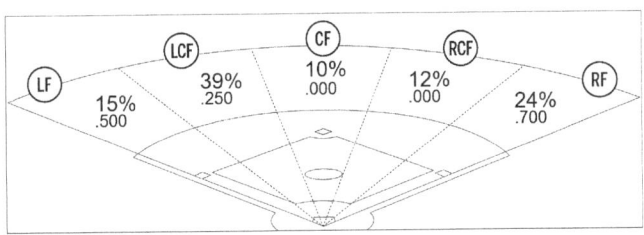

## Strike Zone vs LHP        Strike Zone vs RHP

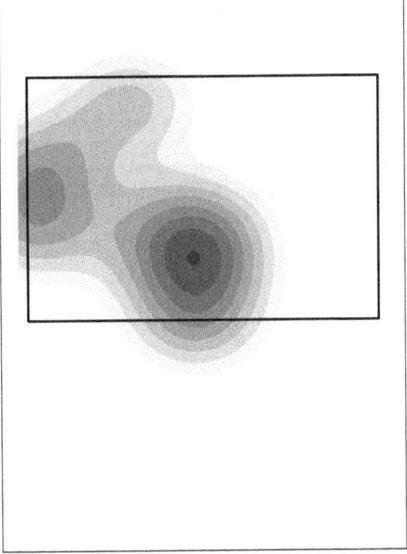

# Cincinnati Reds 2021

## Mike Moustakas  2B

Born: 09/11/88　Age: 32　Bats: L　Throws: R
Height: 6'0"　Weight: 225　Origin: Round 1, 2007 Draft (#2 overall)

| YEAR | TEAM | LVL | AGE | PA | R | 2B | 3B | HR | RBI | BB | K | SB | CS | AVG/OBP/SLG |
|---|---|---|---|---|---|---|---|---|---|---|---|---|---|---|
| 2018 | MIL | MLB | 29 | 218 | 20 | 12 | 0 | 8 | 33 | 19 | 40 | 1 | 1 | .256/.326/.441 |
| 2018 | KC | MLB | 29 | 417 | 46 | 21 | 1 | 20 | 62 | 30 | 63 | 3 | 0 | .249/.309/.468 |
| 2019 | MIL | MLB | 30 | 584 | 80 | 30 | 1 | 35 | 87 | 53 | 98 | 3 | 0 | .254/.329/.516 |
| 2020 | CIN | MLB | 31 | 163 | 13 | 9 | 0 | 8 | 27 | 18 | 36 | 1 | 0 | .230/.331/.468 |
| 2021 FS | CIN | MLB | 32 | 600 | 78 | 27 | 1 | 31 | 90 | 50 | 121 | 2 | 1 | .246/.322/.472 |
| 2021 DC | CIN | MLB | 32 | 578 | 75 | 26 | 1 | 30 | 86 | 48 | 116 | 2 | 1 | .246/.322/.472 |

Comparables: Joe Crede, Scott Brosius, Ty Wigginton

Speaking of third basemen who learned how to hack the keystone, for the first time in his career Moustakas played the majority of his innings at second base. His sure hands and solid fundamentals overcame subpar range to grade out as average defensively, though as Moose is approaching the age where we all lose a few steps, he likely won't be able to keep that up. At the plate Moustakas set a career high in both walk and strikeout rates, which meant he just took a slightly different route to his usual meh-OBP, mmm-SLG offensive destination. He also missed some time with illness and a quad strain, and given the poor health record of second baseman in their 30s Reds fans had best get used to hearing that sort of thing. Moose was worth his multi-million dollar salary last year, but the next few years still look plenty risky.

| YEAR | TEAM | LVL | AGE | PA | DRC+ | BABIP | BRR | FRAA | WARP |
|---|---|---|---|---|---|---|---|---|---|
| 2018 | MIL | MLB | 29 | 218 | 106 | .282 | -2.6 | 3B(52): 0.5 | 0.8 |
| 2018 | KC | MLB | 29 | 417 | 108 | .247 | -2.6 | 3B(76): 11.3, 1B(4): -0.2 | 2.7 |
| 2019 | MIL | MLB | 30 | 584 | 118 | .250 | -2.8 | 3B(105): -0.7, 2B(47): -1.9 | 2.9 |
| 2020 | CIN | MLB | 31 | 163 | 115 | .247 | -0.9 | 2B(32): -3.3, 1B(10): -0.3, 3B(2): 0.2 | 0.3 |
| 2021 FS | CIN | MLB | 32 | 600 | 109 | .265 | -0.7 | 2B -7, 1B 0 | 1.1 |
| 2021 DC | CIN | MLB | 32 | 578 | 109 | .265 | -0.7 | 2B -7, 1B 0 | 1.5 |

*Mike Moustakas, continued*

## Batted Ball Distribution

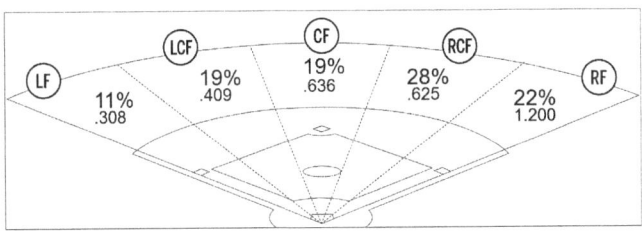

### Strike Zone vs LHP

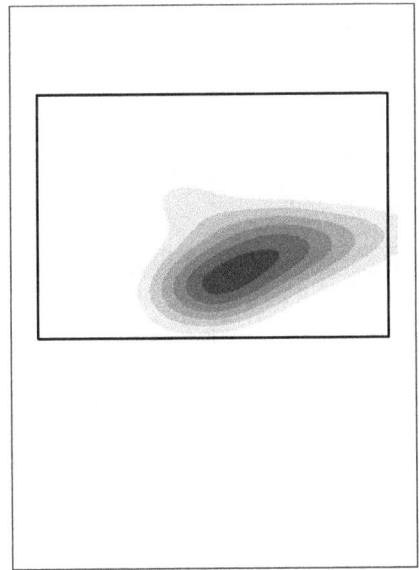

### Strike Zone vs RHP

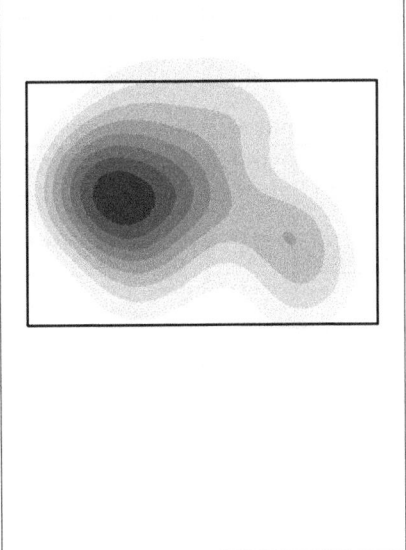

# Cincinnati Reds 2021

## Nick Senzel  CF

Born: 06/29/95   Age: 26   Bats: R   Throws: R
Height: 6'1"   Weight: 205   Origin: Round 1, 2016 Draft (#2 overall)

| YEAR | TEAM | LVL | AGE | PA | R | 2B | 3B | HR | RBI | BB | K | SB | CS | AVG/OBP/SLG |
|---|---|---|---|---|---|---|---|---|---|---|---|---|---|---|
| 2018 | LOU | AAA | 23 | 192 | 23 | 12 | 2 | 6 | 25 | 19 | 39 | 8 | 2 | .312/.380/.512 |
| 2019 | LOU | AAA | 24 | 38 | 7 | 1 | 0 | 1 | 2 | 3 | 13 | 0 | 0 | .257/.316/.371 |
| 2019 | CIN | MLB | 24 | 414 | 55 | 20 | 4 | 12 | 42 | 30 | 101 | 14 | 5 | .256/.315/.427 |
| 2020 | CIN | MLB | 25 | 78 | 8 | 6 | 0 | 2 | 8 | 6 | 15 | 2 | 1 | .186/.247/.357 |
| 2021 FS | CIN | MLB | 26 | 600 | 73 | 24 | 3 | 21 | 72 | 52 | 146 | 11 | 5 | .242/.313/.420 |
| 2021 DC | CIN | MLB | 26 | 471 | 58 | 19 | 2 | 17 | 56 | 40 | 114 | 8 | 4 | .242/.313/.420 |

Comparables: Chris Young, Colby Rasmus, Ryan Thompson

Senzel reported to camp nominally healthy, having recovered from fall shoulder surgery, but as is the norm for his injury-plagued career he didn't remain that way. He hyperextended his elbow in summer camp, sprained a finger, pulled his groin and missed time due to illness on two separate occasions. Along the way he also made a full transition to center field, where his wheels will make him an asset, but struggled mightily at the dish. Senzel makes plenty of contact but has yet to show much power and lofted far too many lazy fly balls last year. The broad set of tools that once made him the second-overall pick can still be seen, but it's hard to say how much of his struggles have been due to his physical ailments and how much is due to him just not being as talented a hitter as we expected. This absolutely could be the year Senzel finally puts it all together and starts earning All-Star votes in the center pasture, but we wouldn't bet on it.

| YEAR | TEAM | LVL | AGE | PA | DRC+ | BABIP | BRR | FRAA | WARP |
|---|---|---|---|---|---|---|---|---|---|
| 2018 | LOU | AAA | 23 | 192 | 150 | .370 | 1.9 | 2B(28): -0.8, 3B(14): 0.8, SS(1): -0.0 | 1.6 |
| 2019 | LOU | AAA | 24 | 38 | 66 | .381 | 0.4 | CF(8): -1.2 | -0.1 |
| 2019 | CIN | MLB | 24 | 414 | 87 | .319 | -0.1 | CF(96): -4.6, 2B(1): 0.0 | 0.4 |
| 2020 | CIN | MLB | 25 | 78 | 99 | .204 | -1.4 | CF(23): 0.1 | 0.0 |
| 2021 FS | CIN | MLB | 26 | 600 | 97 | .292 | 0.7 | CF -1, 2B 0 | 1.5 |
| 2021 DC | CIN | MLB | 26 | 471 | 97 | .292 | 0.5 | CF -1 | 1.3 |

**Nick Senzel,** *continued*

## Batted Ball Distribution

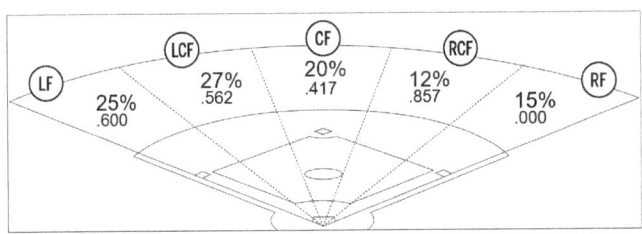

### Strike Zone vs LHP

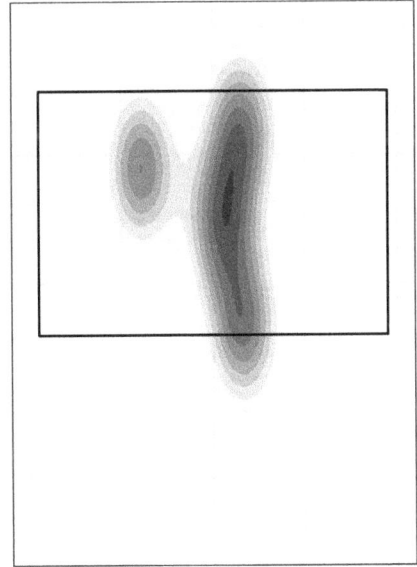

### Strike Zone vs RHP

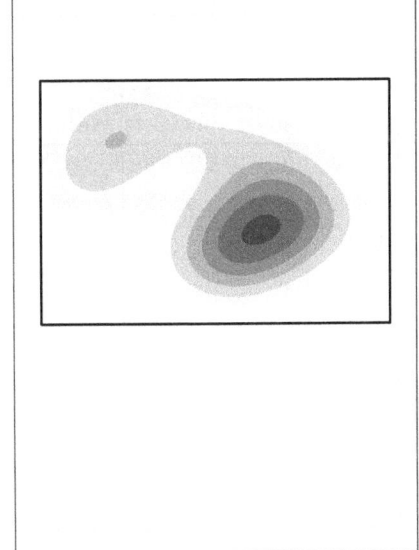

# Cincinnati Reds 2021

## Eugenio Suárez  3B
Born: 07/18/91  Age: 29  Bats: R  Throws: R
Height: 5'11"  Weight: 213  Origin: International Free Agent, 2008

| YEAR | TEAM | LVL | AGE | PA | R | 2B | 3B | HR | RBI | BB | K | SB | CS | AVG/OBP/SLG |
|---|---|---|---|---|---|---|---|---|---|---|---|---|---|---|
| 2018 | CIN | MLB | 26 | 606 | 79 | 22 | 2 | 34 | 104 | 64 | 142 | 1 | 1 | .283/.366/.526 |
| 2019 | CIN | MLB | 27 | 662 | 87 | 22 | 2 | 49 | 103 | 70 | 189 | 3 | 2 | .271/.358/.572 |
| 2020 | CIN | MLB | 28 | 231 | 29 | 8 | 0 | 15 | 38 | 30 | 67 | 2 | 0 | .202/.312/.470 |
| 2021 FS | CIN | MLB | 29 | 600 | 88 | 22 | 1 | 36 | 95 | 67 | 171 | 4 | 3 | .251/.347/.507 |
| 2021 DC | CIN | MLB | 29 | 591 | 87 | 22 | 1 | 35 | 93 | 66 | 168 | 4 | 3 | .251/.347/.507 |

Comparables: Dean Palmer, Wilson Betemit, Jung Ho Kang

    Suárez overcame a horrendous start with a torrid stretch in August and September to put up numbers that would be a good match for his power-packed 2019 breakout, except for that .100 point drop in batting average on balls in play and a small reduction in home runs per fly ball. Back in the buggy-whip days of sabermetrics we may have just described that as bad luck, but now that every ballpark is stuffed with more surveillance devices than Boris Badenov's suitcase, there are oceans of batted ball data to sort through. They show Suárez had pretty much the same profile last year but got under just a few more fly balls, resulting in the small power reduction. He also faced a shift almost 70 percent of the time, way more than in 2019, and struggled against it. Both of those things tend to even out over time, so maybe the lazy, low-tech analysis was just as accurate. With a little luck, Suárez should be back to bombing away as usual this year.

| YEAR | TEAM | LVL | AGE | PA | DRC+ | BABIP | BRR | FRAA | WARP |
|---|---|---|---|---|---|---|---|---|---|
| 2018 | CIN | MLB | 26 | 606 | 136 | .322 | -3.5 | 3B(143): -7.6, SS(3): 0.0 | 3.8 |
| 2019 | CIN | MLB | 27 | 662 | 131 | .312 | -7.9 | 3B(158): 0.1 | 4.4 |
| 2020 | CIN | MLB | 28 | 231 | 112 | .214 | 0.5 | 3B(57): -4.3 | 0.5 |
| 2021 FS | CIN | MLB | 29 | 600 | 125 | .303 | -0.4 | 3B -1, SS 0 | 2.9 |
| 2021 DC | CIN | MLB | 29 | 591 | 125 | .303 | -0.4 | 3B -1 | 2.8 |

*Eugenio Suárez, continued*

## Batted Ball Distribution

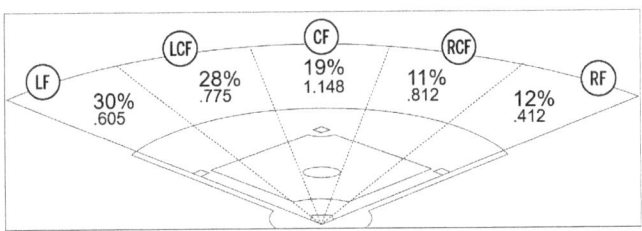

### Strike Zone vs LHP

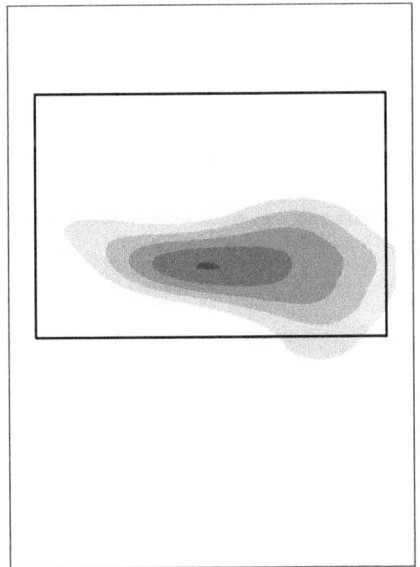

### Strike Zone vs RHP

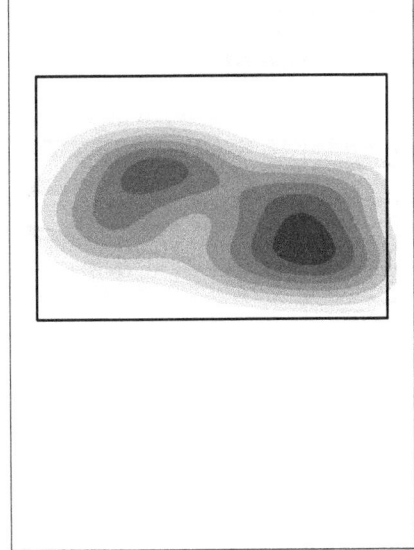

## Joey Votto  1B

Born: 09/10/83   Age: 37   Bats: L   Throws: R
Height: 6'2"   Weight: 220   Origin: Round 2, 2002 Draft (#44 overall)

| YEAR | TEAM | LVL | AGE | PA | R | 2B | 3B | HR | RBI | BB | K | SB | CS | AVG/OBP/SLG |
|---|---|---|---|---|---|---|---|---|---|---|---|---|---|---|
| 2018 | CIN | MLB | 34 | 623 | 67 | 28 | 2 | 12 | 67 | 108 | 101 | 2 | 0 | .284/.417/.419 |
| 2019 | CIN | MLB | 35 | 608 | 79 | 32 | 1 | 15 | 47 | 76 | 123 | 5 | 0 | .261/.357/.411 |
| 2020 | CIN | MLB | 36 | 223 | 32 | 8 | 0 | 11 | 22 | 37 | 43 | 0 | 0 | .226/.354/.446 |
| 2021 FS | CIN | MLB | 37 | 600 | 87 | 23 | 1 | 19 | 67 | 99 | 127 | 4 | 2 | .243/.377/.411 |
| 2021 DC | CIN | MLB | 37 | 611 | 88 | 24 | 1 | 19 | 68 | 101 | 129 | 4 | 2 | .243/.377/.411 |

Comparables: Lance Berkman, Harmon Killebrew, Jeff Bagwell

In mid-August the Reds were struggling to get production from the leadoff spot, eyed up Votto's .378 on-base percentage, and asked the future Hall of Famer to take over at the top of the order. Three weeks, one benching and a .203/.289/.365 line later, Votto was mercifully moved back into the three hole and slashed .250/.409/.596 the rest of the way. "He really doesn't care where he hits," Reds manager David Bell said, but someone should ask Votto's bat what it thinks because a similar experiment in 2019 ended just as tragically. Perhaps it's a subconscious Canadian thing where you don't want to make the pitcher feel bad about himself right off the bat, but whatever the reason, it's probably best to ship that idea off to the Territories for good. Votto is not the legendary lumberman he once was but his batting eye and contact skills are still evident. There's no reason he can't bounce back and post a few more solidly productive years.

| YEAR | TEAM | LVL | AGE | PA | DRC+ | BABIP | BRR | FRAA | WARP |
|---|---|---|---|---|---|---|---|---|---|
| 2018 | CIN | MLB | 34 | 623 | 124 | .333 | -2.6 | 1B(139): 11.6 | 3.7 |
| 2019 | CIN | MLB | 35 | 608 | 108 | .313 | -4.3 | 1B(133): 4.6 | 1.6 |
| 2020 | CIN | MLB | 36 | 223 | 123 | .235 | 1.1 | 1B(50): 3.7 | 1.2 |
| 2021 FS | CIN | MLB | 37 | 600 | 118 | .293 | -0.7 | 1B 5 | 2.7 |
| 2021 DC | CIN | MLB | 37 | 611 | 118 | .293 | -0.7 | 1B 5 | 2.8 |

*Joey Votto, continued*

## Batted Ball Distribution

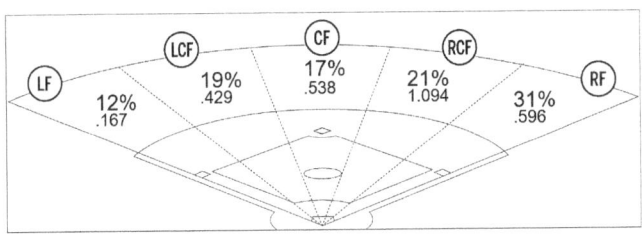

## Strike Zone vs LHP

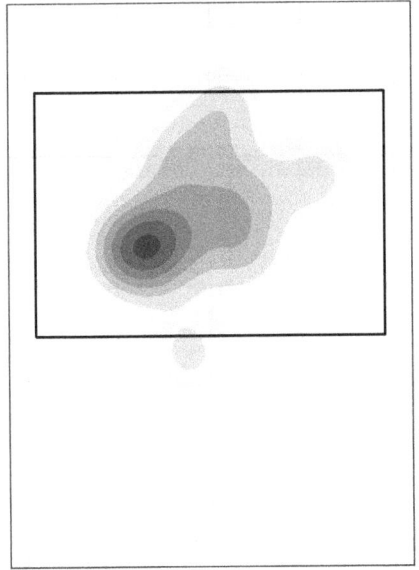

## Strike Zone vs RHP

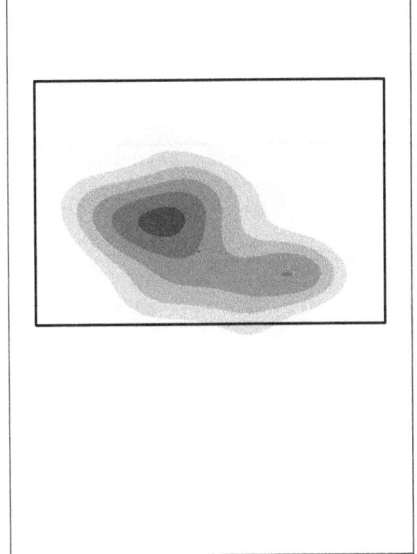

# Cincinnati Reds 2021

## Jesse Winker  LF
Born: 08/17/93  Age: 27  Bats: L  Throws: L
Height: 6'3"  Weight: 215  Origin: Round 1, 2012 Draft (#49 overall)

| YEAR | TEAM | LVL | AGE | PA | R | 2B | 3B | HR | RBI | BB | K | SB | CS | AVG/OBP/SLG |
|---|---|---|---|---|---|---|---|---|---|---|---|---|---|---|
| 2018 | CIN | MLB | 24 | 334 | 38 | 16 | 0 | 7 | 43 | 49 | 46 | 0 | 0 | .299/.405/.431 |
| 2019 | CIN | MLB | 25 | 384 | 51 | 17 | 2 | 16 | 38 | 38 | 60 | 0 | 2 | .269/.357/.473 |
| 2020 | CIN | MLB | 26 | 183 | 27 | 7 | 0 | 12 | 23 | 28 | 46 | 1 | 0 | .255/.388/.544 |
| 2021 FS | CIN | MLB | 27 | 600 | 85 | 25 | 1 | 23 | 75 | 80 | 130 | 1 | 1 | .257/.369/.446 |
| 2021 DC | CIN | MLB | 27 | 492 | 70 | 20 | 1 | 18 | 61 | 65 | 107 | 1 | 1 | .257/.369/.446 |

Comparables: Rusty Greer, Carmelo Martinez, Gary Roenicke

Yeah, we know, correlation is not causation, but it's interesting to note that the first time Winker was able to stay healthy for a full season was also the only season he could spend considerable time as the designated hitter. It was also a short season, so there's no knowing whether Winker would have stayed upright through a full slate of games, but in any case it all came together last year for the lanky lefty. Winker managed to display both patience and power at the same time and finally did some damage against portside pitching, albeit in a very small sample. He even seemed more comfortable in the outfield when he did don his glove. This is the Winker we had only seen glimpses of before but knew existed, and if he can avoid injury during his prime expect him to be a lineup force for years to come.

| YEAR | TEAM | LVL | AGE | PA | DRC+ | BABIP | BRR | FRAA | WARP |
|---|---|---|---|---|---|---|---|---|---|
| 2018 | CIN | MLB | 24 | 334 | 117 | .336 | -2.6 | RF(47): -1.0, LF(34): -3.5 | 0.8 |
| 2019 | CIN | MLB | 25 | 384 | 114 | .286 | 0.6 | LF(72): 1.4, CF(21): 0.0, RF(18): 1.6 | 2.2 |
| 2020 | CIN | MLB | 26 | 183 | 125 | .283 | -0.2 | LF(15): 1.0, RF(1): -0.2 | 1.1 |
| 2021 FS | CIN | MLB | 27 | 600 | 122 | .306 | -0.9 | LF 0, CF 0 | 3.1 |
| 2021 DC | CIN | MLB | 27 | 492 | 122 | .306 | -0.8 | LF 0 | 2.2 |

*Jesse Winker, continued*

## Batted Ball Distribution

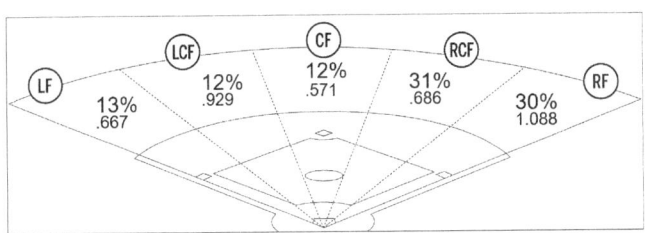

## Strike Zone vs LHP    Strike Zone vs RHP

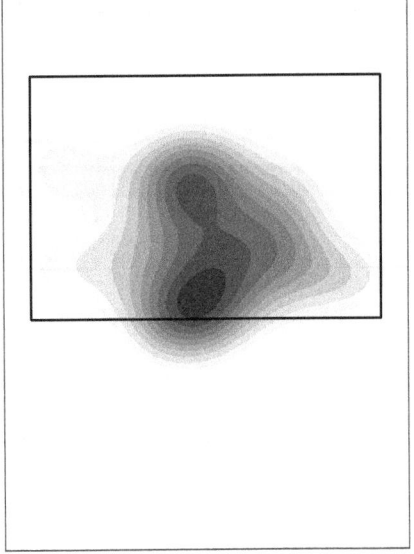

# Cincinnati Reds 2021

## Tejay Antone   RHP
Born: 12/05/93   Age: 27   Bats: R   Throws: R
Height: 6'4"   Weight: 230   Origin: Round 5, 2014 Draft (#155 overall)

| YEAR | TEAM | LVL | AGE | W | L | SV | G | GS | IP | H | HR | BB/9 | K/9 | K | GB% | BABIP |
|---|---|---|---|---|---|---|---|---|---|---|---|---|---|---|---|---|
| 2018 | DAY | HI-A | 24 | 6 | 3 | 0 | 17 | 17 | 96 | 95 | 6 | 2.7 | 7.7 | 82 | 47.1% | .308 |
| 2019 | CHA | AA | 25 | 7 | 4 | 0 | 13 | 13 | 74² | 63 | 4 | 2.7 | 7.6 | 63 | 56.8% | .277 |
| 2019 | LOU | AAA | 25 | 4 | 8 | 0 | 14 | 13 | 71² | 93 | 7 | 3.9 | 8.8 | 70 | 51.1% | .402 |
| 2020 | CIN | MLB | 26 | 0 | 3 | 0 | 13 | 4 | 35¹ | 20 | 4 | 4.1 | 11.5 | 45 | 48.7% | .216 |
| 2021 FS | CIN | MLB | 27 | 9 | 8 | 0 | 26 | 26 | 150 | 134 | 19 | 4.1 | 9.0 | 150 | 50.3% | .287 |
| 2021 DC | CIN | MLB | 27 | 9 | 7 | 0 | 44 | 21 | 123.7 | 111 | 15 | 4.1 | 9.0 | 124 | 50.3% | .287 |

Comparables: Scott Barlow, Jake Esch, Chase De Jong

Antone possesses Jake Arrieta's frame and beard but never really resembled a true power pitcher until training at the APEC facility in Texas during the 2019-20 offseason. The work he put in transformed his mundane two-seamer into a high-spin demon that can reach the high-90s, and his curveball and slider improved into plus offerings. Antone impressed in the spring, dominated in the Reds bullpen last summer and even made four starts. His strikeout rate was elite, though a few extra walks shoulder-surfed their way in and caused his numbers to be far better when he worked in relief. The Reds hope Antone can gain a little more command of his newfound arsenal and make another go at cracking the rotation, but at a minimum they've found a late-blooming and versatile weapon.

| YEAR | TEAM | LVL | AGE | WHIP | ERA | DRA- | WARP | MPH | FB% | WHF | CSP |
|---|---|---|---|---|---|---|---|---|---|---|---|
| 2018 | DAY | HI-A | 24 | 1.29 | 4.03 | 98 | 0.6 | | | | |
| 2019 | CHA | AA | 25 | 1.14 | 3.38 | 86 | 0.7 | | | | |
| 2019 | LOU | AAA | 25 | 1.73 | 4.65 | 134 | 0.1 | | | | |
| 2020 | CIN | MLB | 26 | 1.02 | 2.80 | 80 | 0.7 | 97.6 | 40.5% | 34.4% | |
| 2021 FS | CIN | MLB | 27 | 1.36 | 4.02 | 91 | 2.2 | 97.6 | 40.5% | 34.4% | 44.2% |
| 2021 DC | CIN | MLB | 27 | 1.36 | 4.02 | 91 | 1.5 | 97.6 | 40.5% | 34.4% | 44.2% |

*Tejay Antone, continued*

## Pitch Shape vs LHH

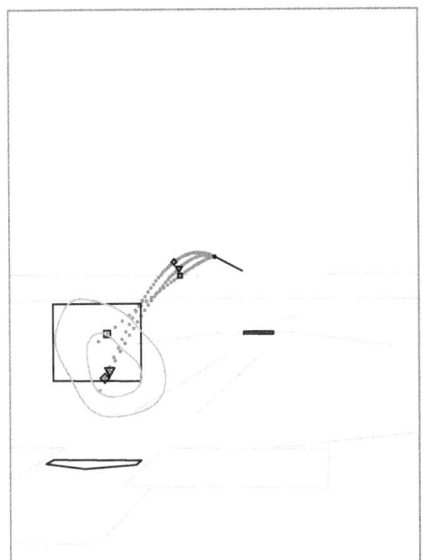

## Pitch Shape vs RHH

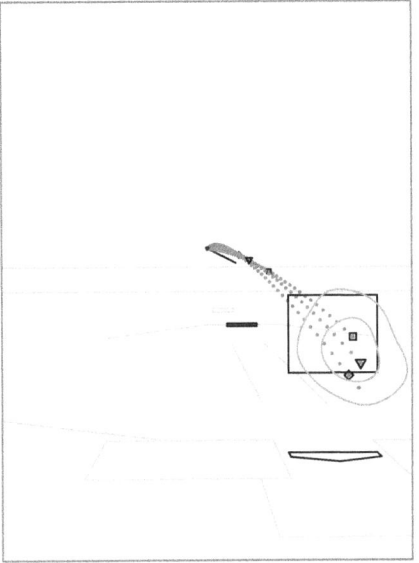

| Type | Frequency | Velocity | H Movement | V Movement |
|---|---|---|---|---|
| ☐ Sinker | 38.4% | 95.9 [118] | -10 [122] | -16 [115] |
| ▽ Slider | 39.8% | 83.7 [99] | 6.2 [104] | -35.7 [94] |
| ◇ Curveball | 16.7% | 80.3 [106] | 14.5 [128] | -47.8 [101] |

# Cincinnati Reds 2021

## Cam Bedrosian  RHP
Born: 10/02/91   Age: 29   Bats: R   Throws: R
Height: 6'1"   Weight: 225   Origin: Round 1, 2010 Draft (#29 overall)

| YEAR | TEAM | LVL | AGE | W | L | SV | G | GS | IP | H | HR | BB/9 | K/9 | K | GB% | BABIP |
|---|---|---|---|---|---|---|---|---|---|---|---|---|---|---|---|---|
| 2018 | LAA | MLB | 26 | 5 | 4 | 1 | 71 | 0 | 64 | 63 | 7 | 3.7 | 8.0 | 57 | 48.1% | .316 |
| 2019 | LAA | MLB | 27 | 3 | 3 | 1 | 59 | 7 | 61$^1$ | 48 | 7 | 3.2 | 9.4 | 64 | 48.5% | .253 |
| 2020 | LAA | MLB | 28 | 0 | 0 | 0 | 11 | 0 | 14$^2$ | 10 | 0 | 3.7 | 6.8 | 11 | 31.7% | .244 |
| 2021 FS | CIN | MLB | 29 | 2 | 2 | 0 | 57 | 0 | 50 | 46 | 8 | 3.7 | 9.2 | 51 | 43.4% | .286 |

Comparables: Arodys Vizcaíno, Dominic Leone, Jorge Julio

Much as a first-round flamethrower ending up in the bullpen will always spell disappointment to some, "Bedrock" nevertheless lived up to the sobriquet in his seven-year career with the Angels—apparently at an end after the team outrighted him in October. Though never consistent enough to decisively move to the *above-* half of average, even as he bled velocity, the major league scion was an integral, steadying presence to an Angels bullpen getting repackaged more often than the Nintendo 3DS. The penny-pinching financial landscape magnified what might be either short-season strangeness or declining stuff—MLB has room yet for relievers striking out 6.8 batters per nine, but maybe not of Bedrosian's ilk. If there's any comfort to be had, it's that his head start out the door of the Angels' bullpen was a short one, given that the rest got non-tendered in a fit of planned obsolescence less than two months later.

| YEAR | TEAM | LVL | AGE | WHIP | ERA | DRA- | WARP | MPH | FB% | WHF | CSP |
|---|---|---|---|---|---|---|---|---|---|---|---|
| 2018 | LAA | MLB | 26 | 1.39 | 3.80 | 93 | 0.5 | 95.1 | 55.5% | 22.0% | |
| 2019 | LAA | MLB | 27 | 1.14 | 3.23 | 71 | 1.3 | 94.5 | 47.8% | 30.3% | |
| 2020 | LAA | MLB | 28 | 1.09 | 2.45 | 112 | 0.0 | 93.9 | 52.7% | 22.9% | |
| 2021 FS | CIN | MLB | 29 | 1.34 | 4.25 | 96 | 0.3 | 94.5 | 50.9% | 26.6% | 46.8% |

*Cam Bedrosian, continued*

### Pitch Shape vs LHH

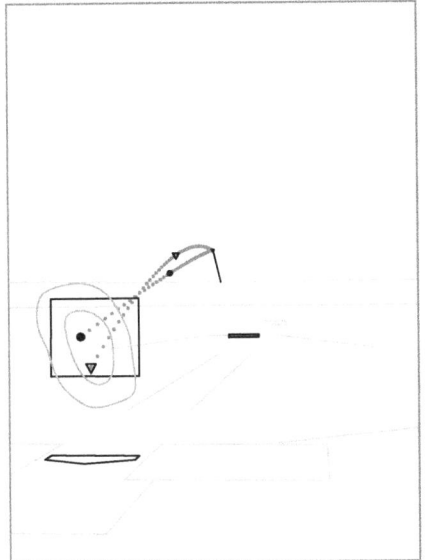

### Pitch Shape vs RHH

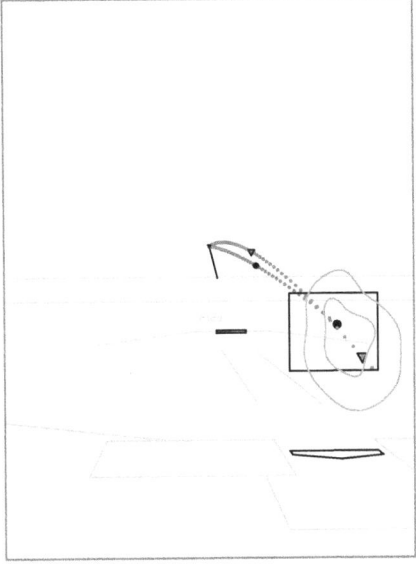

| Type | Frequency | Velocity | H Movement | V Movement |
|---|---|---|---|---|
| ● Fastball | 52.7% | 92.3 [99] | -4.2 [112] | -11.2 [111] |
| ▽ Slider | 46.1% | 81.3 [88] | 4.3 [97] | -43.6 [71] |

## Luis Castillo   RHP

Born: 12/12/92   Age: 28   Bats: R   Throws: R
Height: 6'2"   Weight: 200   Origin: International Free Agent, 2012

| YEAR | TEAM | LVL | AGE | W | L | SV | G | GS | IP | H | HR | BB/9 | K/9 | K | GB% | BABIP |
|---|---|---|---|---|---|---|---|---|---|---|---|---|---|---|---|---|
| 2018 | CIN | MLB | 25 | 10 | 12 | 0 | 32 | 32 | 173² | 164 | 28 | 2.6 | 8.8 | 169 | 46.4% | .288 |
| 2019 | CIN | MLB | 26 | 15 | 8 | 0 | 32 | 32 | 190² | 139 | 22 | 3.7 | 10.7 | 226 | 54.6% | .265 |
| 2020 | CIN | MLB | 27 | 4 | 6 | 0 | 12 | 12 | 70 | 62 | 5 | 3.1 | 11.4 | 89 | 58.4% | .329 |
| 2021 FS | CIN | MLB | 28 | 10 | 7 | 0 | 26 | 26 | 150 | 123 | 16 | 3.6 | 10.7 | 177 | 54.2% | .290 |
| 2021 DC | CIN | MLB | 28 | 12 | 8 | 0 | 29 | 29 | 172 | 141 | 19 | 3.6 | 10.7 | 203 | 54.2% | .290 |

Comparables: Aaron Nola, Danny Salazar, Nick Pivetta

There's no question that Castillo has top-shelf stuff that rivals any starter in the game. His fastball sits comfortably in the high 90s, his slider generates plenty of empty swings and his legendary changeup is effective against both righties and lefties. Yet Castillo has not yet put together an award-worthy effort to match the Coles, deGroms and Biebers that surround him on the swinging-strike leaderboard. Perhaps it's pitch selection, perhaps it's experience, perhaps it's just luck. Last spring our own Matthew Trueblood suggested a liberal application of the slider to help address his platoon issues and Castillo actually did break it out a little more often, but lefties slugged .583 against it. However that plays out in the long run, Castillo seems to be just one tweak away from making his whole at least equal to the sum of his parts. Once that happens the hardware will follow.

| YEAR | TEAM | LVL | AGE | WHIP | ERA | DRA- | WARP | MPH | FB% | WHF | CSP |
|---|---|---|---|---|---|---|---|---|---|---|---|
| 2018 | CIN | MLB | 25 | 1.23 | 4.40 | 106 | 1.1 | 97.8 | 57.2% | 28.8% | |
| 2019 | CIN | MLB | 26 | 1.14 | 3.40 | 61 | 5.7 | 98.1 | 50.6% | 35.9% | |
| 2020 | CIN | MLB | 27 | 1.23 | 3.21 | 59 | 2.2 | 98.8 | 52.3% | 32.8% | |
| 2021 FS | CIN | MLB | 28 | 1.23 | 3.21 | 76 | 3.4 | 98.2 | 52.5% | 33.4% | 44.3% |
| 2021 DC | CIN | MLB | 28 | 1.23 | 3.21 | 76 | 3.9 | 98.2 | 52.5% | 33.4% | 44.3% |

*Luis Castillo, continued*

## Pitch Shape vs LHH

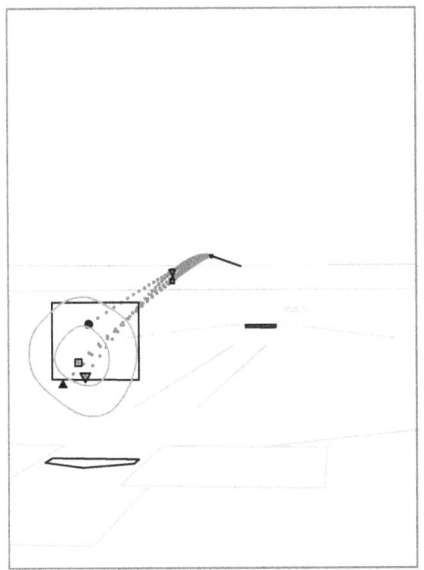

## Pitch Shape vs RHH

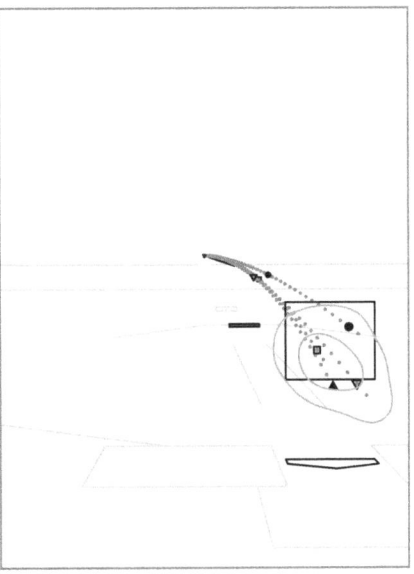

| Type | Frequency | Velocity | H Movement | V Movement |
|---|---|---|---|---|
| ● Fastball | 27.0% | 97.6 [116] | -9.8 [85] | -14.7 [101] |
| □ Sinker | 25.3% | 97.7 [127] | -16 [78] | -22 [95] |
| ▲ Changeup | 30.0% | 88.4 [113] | -14.7 [84] | -30.4 [92] |
| ▽ Slider | 17.7% | 86.9 [113] | 0 [80] | -31.9 [105] |

## José De León  RHP

Born: 08/07/92   Age: 28   Bats: R   Throws: R
Height: 6'2"   Weight: 215   Origin: Round 24, 2013 Draft (#724 overall)

| YEAR | TEAM | LVL | AGE | W | L | SV | G | GS | IP | H | HR | BB/9 | K/9 | K | GB% | BABIP |
|---|---|---|---|---|---|---|---|---|---|---|---|---|---|---|---|---|
| 2019 | DUR | AAA | 26 | 2 | 1 | 1 | 17 | 13 | 51[1] | 41 | 4 | 4.7 | 12.8 | 73 | 30.2% | .330 |
| 2019 | TB | MLB | 26 | 1 | 0 | 0 | 3 | 0 | 4 | 3 | 0 | 6.8 | 15.8 | 7 | 44.4% | .333 |
| 2020 | CIN | MLB | 27 | 0 | 0 | 0 | 5 | 0 | 6 | 6 | 1 | 16.5 | 15.0 | 10 | 42.9% | .385 |
| 2021 FS | CIN | MLB | 28 | 2 | 2 | 0 | 57 | 0 | 50 | 44 | 8 | 4.6 | 10.6 | 58 | 35.1% | .293 |
| 2021 DC | CIN | MLB | 28 | 4 | 4 | 0 | 41 | 6 | 44.3 | 39 | 7 | 4.6 | 10.6 | 52 | 35.1% | .293 |

Comparables: Ben Lively, Daniel Mengden, Dinelson Lamet

De León survived his Tommy John surgery in a literal sense, but his career remains in critical condition after walking almost a third of the batters he faced last year; he still can crank out mid-90s fastballs and Bugs Bunny changeups, but until he regains some sense of where they're going he's not going anywhere.

| YEAR | TEAM | LVL | AGE | WHIP | ERA | DRA- | WARP | MPH | FB% | WHF | CSP |
|---|---|---|---|---|---|---|---|---|---|---|---|
| 2019 | DUR | AAA | 26 | 1.32 | 3.51 | 78 | 1.4 | | | | |
| 2019 | TB | MLB | 26 | 1.50 | 2.25 | 63 | 0.1 | 94.8 | 57.5% | 45.0% | |
| 2020 | CIN | MLB | 27 | 2.83 | 18.00 | 95 | 0.1 | 96.9 | 69.3% | 37.7% | |
| 2021 FS | CIN | MLB | 28 | 1.41 | 4.65 | 101 | 0.2 | 96.3 | 66.0% | 39.7% | 45.1% |
| 2021 DC | CIN | MLB | 28 | 1.41 | 4.65 | 101 | 0.2 | 96.3 | 66.0% | 39.7% | 45.1% |

*José De León, continued*

## Pitch Shape vs LHH

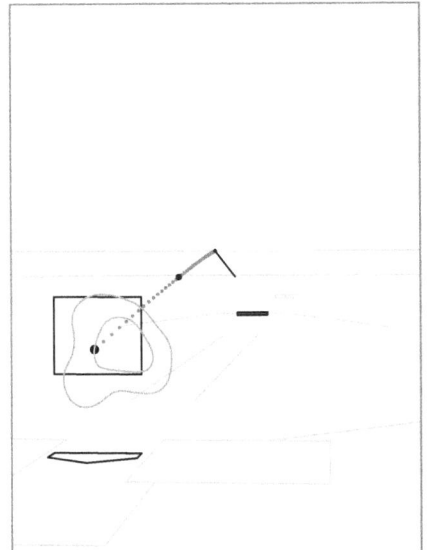

## Pitch Shape vs RHH

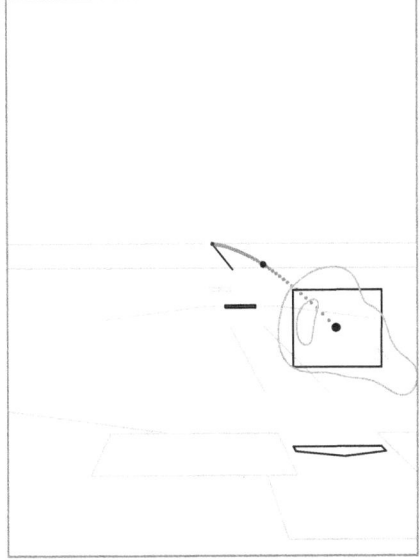

| Type | Frequency | Velocity | H Movement | V Movement |
|---|---|---|---|---|
| ● Fastball | 66.0% | 95.2 [108] | -9.8 [85] | -13.6 [105] |
| ▲ Changeup | 21.1% | 86.2 [104] | -12.4 [96] | -30 [93] |
| ▽ Slider | 8.2% | 83.3 [97] | 12 [126] | -31.8 [106] |

# Cincinnati Reds 2021

## Sean Doolittle  LHP

Born: 09/26/86   Age: 34   Bats: L   Throws: L
Height: 6'2"   Weight: 204   Origin: Round 1, 2007 Draft (#41 overall)

| YEAR | TEAM | LVL | AGE | W | L | SV | G | GS | IP | H | HR | BB/9 | K/9 | K | GB% | BABIP |
|---|---|---|---|---|---|---|---|---|---|---|---|---|---|---|---|---|
| 2018 | WAS | MLB | 31 | 3 | 3 | 25 | 43 | 0 | 45 | 21 | 3 | 1.2 | 12.0 | 60 | 31.6% | .196 |
| 2019 | WAS | MLB | 32 | 6 | 5 | 29 | 63 | 0 | 60 | 63 | 11 | 2.2 | 9.9 | 66 | 24.9% | .315 |
| 2020 | WAS | MLB | 33 | 0 | 2 | 0 | 11 | 0 | 7² | 9 | 3 | 4.7 | 7.0 | 6 | 3.8% | .273 |
| 2021 FS | CIN | MLB | 34 | 2 | 2 | 22 | 57 | 0 | 50 | 42 | 9 | 2.0 | 8.8 | 49 | 27.3% | .258 |
| 2021 DC | CIN | MLB | 34 | 2 | 2 | 22 | 56 | 0 | 49 | 41 | 8 | 2.0 | 8.8 | 48 | 27.3% | .258 |

Comparables: Nick Vincent, Kirby Yates, Tommy Hunter

We hear drums, drums in the deep. Sliders are coming. Doolittle is best known as a one-pitch pitcher—you don't need a trash can to know he's probably going to throw a low-to-mid-90s fastball high in the zone. He hasn't thrown a curveball since 2014, and his slider and changeup usage each lingered in single digits throughout his big-league career. With his velocity dipping in 2020, Doolittle threw more sliders, and to decent effect (albeit over a small sample). There are two obvious paths forward ahead of him: one involves regaining his velocity, the other entails improving his slider to give him another weapon. We'll see which way Doolittle goes; we just hope that one of the most likable players in the game can find a way to enjoy more success heading forward.

| YEAR | TEAM | LVL | AGE | WHIP | ERA | DRA- | WARP | MPH | FB% | WHF | CSP |
|---|---|---|---|---|---|---|---|---|---|---|---|
| 2018 | WAS | MLB | 31 | 0.60 | 1.60 | 66 | 1.0 | 95.7 | 88.8% | 33.8% | |
| 2019 | WAS | MLB | 32 | 1.30 | 4.05 | 100 | 0.3 | 95.2 | 88.2% | 23.5% | |
| 2020 | WAS | MLB | 33 | 1.70 | 5.87 | 166 | -0.2 | 92.2 | 81.9% | 18.7% | |
| 2021 FS | CIN | MLB | 34 | 1.06 | 3.16 | 76 | 0.9 | 95.0 | 87.5% | 25.0% | 50.6% |
| 2021 DC | CIN | MLB | 34 | 1.06 | 3.16 | 76 | 0.9 | 95.0 | 87.5% | 25.0% | 50.6% |

**Sean Doolittle, continued**

## Pitch Shape vs LHH

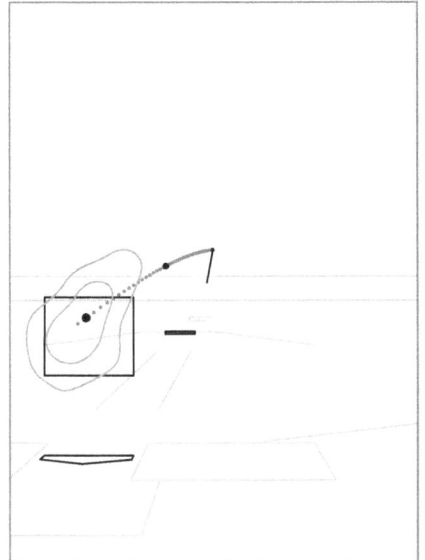

## Pitch Shape vs RHH

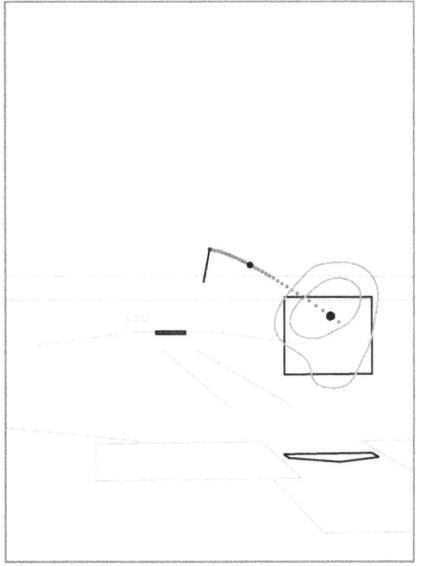

| Type | Frequency | Velocity | H Movement | V Movement |
|---|---|---|---|---|
| ● Fastball | 77.6% | 90.9 [95] | 3 [118] | -12.6 [107] |
| ▲ Changeup | 5.2% | 81.4 [85] | 11.1 [104] | -23.6 [111] |
| ▽ Slider | 11.9% | 80.8 [86] | -6.1 [103] | -32.7 [103] |

# Cincinnati Reds 2021

## Amir Garrett  LHP

Born: 05/03/92   Age: 29   Bats: R   Throws: L
Height: 6'5"   Weight: 239   Origin: Round 22, 2011 Draft (#685 overall)

| YEAR | TEAM | LVL | AGE | W | L | SV | G | GS | IP | H | HR | BB/9 | K/9 | K | GB% | BABIP |
|---|---|---|---|---|---|---|---|---|---|---|---|---|---|---|---|---|
| 2018 | CIN | MLB | 26 | 1 | 2 | 0 | 66 | 0 | 63 | 56 | 8 | 3.6 | 10.1 | 71 | 38.2% | .308 |
| 2019 | CIN | MLB | 27 | 5 | 3 | 0 | 69 | 0 | 56 | 44 | 7 | 5.6 | 12.5 | 78 | 54.3% | .303 |
| 2020 | CIN | MLB | 28 | 1 | 0 | 1 | 21 | 0 | 18$^1$ | 10 | 4 | 3.4 | 12.8 | 26 | 44.4% | .188 |
| 2021 FS | CIN | MLB | 29 | 2 | 2 | 11 | 57 | 0 | 50 | 41 | 6 | 4.6 | 11.5 | 63 | 45.1% | .294 |
| 2021 DC | CIN | MLB | 29 | 2 | 2 | 11 | 53 | 0 | 55.3 | 45 | 7 | 4.6 | 11.5 | 70 | 45.1% | .294 |

Comparables: Dylan Covey, Adam Plutko, Steven Brault

Garrett uses a pitching mound the same way Clark Kent uses a phone booth. In goes the mild-mannered Amir and out comes AG, who pitches with intensity, passion and the best strikeout scream in baseball. AG can dominate same-side hitters with his lethal fastball/slider combo, allowing them just one single in 28 at-bats last year, but patient righty bats can feast on the occasional mistake, rendering him better suited to a set-up role than the ninth inning. AG's boisterous energy can be infectious between the lines, but Amir helped his teammates just as much in the clubhouse last summer by quietly sharing his experiences growing up Black in the United States. It's sometimes easy to forget that ballparks are ultimately a workplace, and both Amir and AG have important roles to play there.

| YEAR | TEAM | LVL | AGE | WHIP | ERA | DRA- | WARP | MPH | FB% | WHF | CSP |
|---|---|---|---|---|---|---|---|---|---|---|---|
| 2018 | CIN | MLB | 26 | 1.29 | 4.29 | 98 | 0.4 | 97.2 | 63.2% | 32.0% | |
| 2019 | CIN | MLB | 27 | 1.41 | 3.21 | 68 | 1.2 | 97.3 | 42.0% | 39.0% | |
| 2020 | CIN | MLB | 28 | 0.93 | 2.45 | 81 | 0.4 | 97.0 | 44.5% | 43.7% | |
| 2021 FS | CIN | MLB | 29 | 1.34 | 3.87 | 88 | 0.6 | 97.2 | 48.2% | 38.2% | 42.9% |
| 2021 DC | CIN | MLB | 29 | 1.34 | 3.87 | 88 | 0.7 | 97.2 | 48.2% | 38.2% | 42.9% |

*Amir Garrett, continued*

## Pitch Shape vs LHH

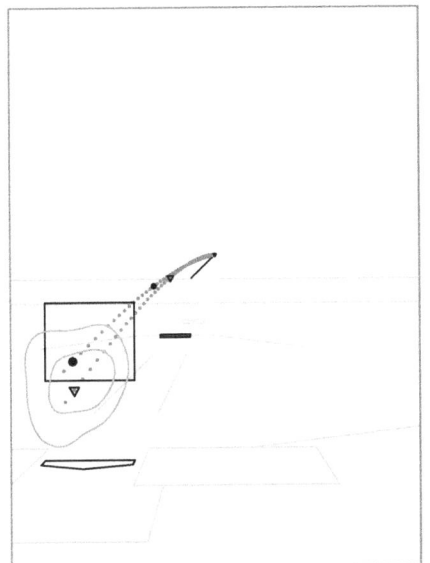

## Pitch Shape vs RHH

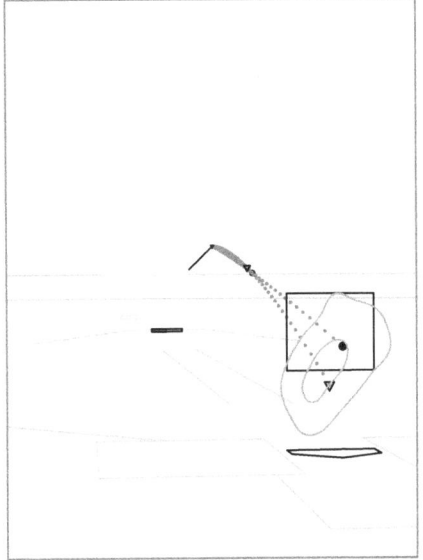

| Type | Frequency | Velocity | H Movement | V Movement |
|---|---|---|---|---|
| ● Fastball | 39.1% | 95 [108] | 9.8 [85] | -14.4 [102] |
| ☐ Sinker | 5.4% | 94.5 [111] | 14.4 [90] | -19.1 [105] |
| ▽ Slider | 55.5% | 85.3 [106] | -0.3 [81] | -30.8 [108] |

## Sonny Gray  RHP

Born: 11/07/89  Age: 31  Bats: R  Throws: R
Height: 5'10"  Weight: 195  Origin: Round 1, 2011 Draft (#18 overall)

| YEAR | TEAM | LVL | AGE | W | L | SV | G | GS | IP | H | HR | BB/9 | K/9 | K | GB% | BABIP |
|---|---|---|---|---|---|---|---|---|---|---|---|---|---|---|---|---|
| 2018 | NYY | MLB | 28 | 11 | 9 | 0 | 30 | 23 | 130¹ | 138 | 14 | 3.9 | 8.5 | 123 | 50.5% | .327 |
| 2019 | CIN | MLB | 29 | 11 | 8 | 0 | 31 | 31 | 175¹ | 122 | 17 | 3.5 | 10.5 | 204 | 50.5% | .259 |
| 2020 | CIN | MLB | 30 | 5 | 3 | 0 | 11 | 11 | 56 | 42 | 4 | 4.2 | 11.6 | 72 | 51.9% | .290 |
| 2021 FS | CIN | MLB | 31 | 10 | 7 | 0 | 26 | 26 | 150 | 130 | 20 | 4.0 | 10.4 | 173 | 50.5% | .295 |
| 2021 DC | CIN | MLB | 31 | 11 | 8 | 0 | 29 | 29 | 166 | 144 | 22 | 4.0 | 10.4 | 192 | 50.5% | .295 |

Comparables: Chris Archer, Jake Odorizzi, Zack Wheeler

New York is a notoriously tough place for men named Sonny, whether real or fictional. Sonny Corleone was ambushed at a tollbooth and brought down in a hail of gunfire. Sonny Red was jumped and murdered in his own basement by a crew led by Sonny Black, who was in turn betrayed by undercover FBI agent Joe Pistone. Sonny Gray's unfortunate Bronx sojourn didn't end quite so dramatically, but putting Yankee Stadium in his rear-view mirror has placed his career back in the fast lane. Since arriving in Cincinnati two seasons ago, Gray is once again pitching like the frontline starter he had been in Oakland. He uses five pitches to keep hitters off-balance, spotting sinkers and four-seamers in on the hands before getting righties to chase his slider low-and-away or fooling lefties with his hammer curve or the occasional *cambio*. Of course, the same pitches with a similar approach face-planted in pinstripes, so should the Reds be concerned Gray might suddenly turn back into a pumpkin? Fuhgeddaboudit.

| YEAR | TEAM | LVL | AGE | WHIP | ERA | DRA- | WARP | MPH | FB% | WHF | CSP |
|---|---|---|---|---|---|---|---|---|---|---|---|
| 2018 | NYY | MLB | 28 | 1.50 | 4.90 | 111 | 0.4 | 95.2 | 57.2% | 25.2% | |
| 2019 | CIN | MLB | 29 | 1.08 | 2.87 | 61 | 5.3 | 94.9 | 50.5% | 28.2% | |
| 2020 | CIN | MLB | 30 | 1.21 | 3.70 | 75 | 1.3 | 94.5 | 55.4% | 29.6% | |
| 2021 FS | CIN | MLB | 31 | 1.31 | 3.81 | 87 | 2.5 | 94.8 | 53.2% | 28.0% | 43.2% |
| 2021 DC | CIN | MLB | 31 | 1.31 | 3.81 | 87 | 2.8 | 94.8 | 53.2% | 28.0% | 43.2% |

*Sonny Gray, continued*

## Pitch Shape vs LHH

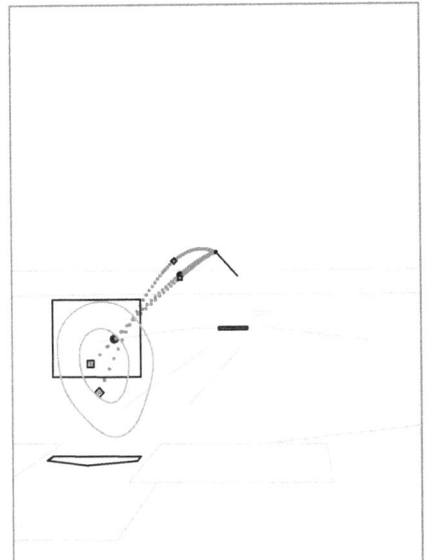

## Pitch Shape vs RHH

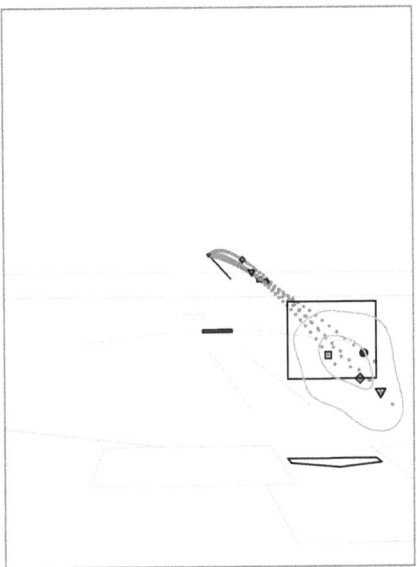

| Type | Frequency | Velocity | H Movement | V Movement |
|---|---|---|---|---|
| ● Fastball | 25.4% | 93.3 [102] | -1.9 [123] | -14.2 [103] |
| □ Sinker | 29.6% | 92.9 [103] | -11.6 [111] | -19.1 [105] |
| ▽ Slider | 15.6% | 83.2 [97] | 15.1 [137] | -40.5 [80] |
| ◇ Curveball | 28.2% | 81 [109] | 13.7 [125] | -48.9 [99] |

# Cincinnati Reds 2021

## Jeff Hoffman  RHP
Born: 01/08/93  Age: 28  Bats: R  Throws: R
Height: 6'5"  Weight: 235  Origin: Round 1, 2014 Draft (#9 overall)

| YEAR | TEAM | LVL | AGE | W | L | SV | G | GS | IP | H | HR | BB/9 | K/9 | K | GB% | BABIP |
|---|---|---|---|---|---|---|---|---|---|---|---|---|---|---|---|---|
| 2018 | ABQ | AAA | 25 | 6 | 8 | 0 | 21 | 21 | 105.2 | 105 | 9 | 4.0 | 8.7 | 102 | 44.1% | .334 |
| 2018 | COL | MLB | 25 | 0 | 0 | 0 | 6 | 1 | 8.2 | 15 | 0 | 7.3 | 5.2 | 5 | 53.1% | .469 |
| 2019 | ABQ | AAA | 26 | 6 | 8 | 0 | 17 | 16 | 85.1 | 105 | 19 | 3.2 | 10.3 | 98 | 42.4% | .363 |
| 2019 | COL | MLB | 26 | 2 | 6 | 0 | 15 | 15 | 70 | 77 | 21 | 4.4 | 8.7 | 68 | 34.9% | .303 |
| 2020 | COL | MLB | 27 | 2 | 1 | 1 | 16 | 0 | 21.1 | 32 | 3 | 3.8 | 8.4 | 20 | 35.6% | .414 |
| 2021 FS | CIN | MLB | 28 | 2 | 3 | 0 | 57 | 0 | 50 | 50 | 9 | 3.9 | 8.6 | 47 | 39.5% | .294 |
| 2021 DC | CIN | MLB | 28 | 2 | 2 | 0 | 47 | 0 | 49 | 49 | 9 | 3.9 | 8.6 | 47 | 39.5% | .294 |

Comparables: Daniel Mengden, Robert Stephenson, Erick Fedde

His combination of prolific prospect status and poor results may lead one to believe that Hoffman is a left-handed pitcher, and you would have good reason to think that—right-handers have eaten him alive like an elementary school tour of a Goldfish cracker factory. He's faced over 500 right-handed batters in the majors and they have a 1.000 OPS against him; nobody's ever been that bad against righties for that long as a fellow northpaw. The Rockies shifted him to mid-inning duties and it didn't help, because he throws the same fastball in those innings for batters to hammer all over the metropolitan area. Maybe he really is left-handed and forgot. He'll try to recall his handedness and one-time dominance in Cincinnati.

| YEAR | TEAM | LVL | AGE | WHIP | ERA | DRA- | WARP | MPH | FB% | WHF | CSP |
|---|---|---|---|---|---|---|---|---|---|---|---|
| 2018 | ABQ | AAA | 25 | 1.44 | 4.94 | 89 | 1.6 | | | | |
| 2018 | COL | MLB | 25 | 2.54 | 9.35 | 161 | -0.2 | 94.7 | 53.9% | 18.5% | |
| 2019 | ABQ | AAA | 26 | 1.58 | 7.70 | 113 | 1.0 | | | | |
| 2019 | COL | MLB | 26 | 1.59 | 6.56 | 142 | -0.9 | 95.6 | 58.8% | 21.7% | |
| 2020 | COL | MLB | 27 | 1.92 | 9.28 | 113 | 0.0 | 96.5 | 54.6% | 22.2% | |
| 2021 FS | CIN | MLB | 28 | 1.43 | 5.09 | 110 | 0.0 | 95.8 | 57.3% | 21.7% | 47.1% |
| 2021 DC | CIN | MLB | 28 | 1.43 | 5.09 | 110 | 0.0 | 95.8 | 57.3% | 21.7% | 47.1% |

*Jeff Hoffman, continued*

## Pitch Shape vs LHH

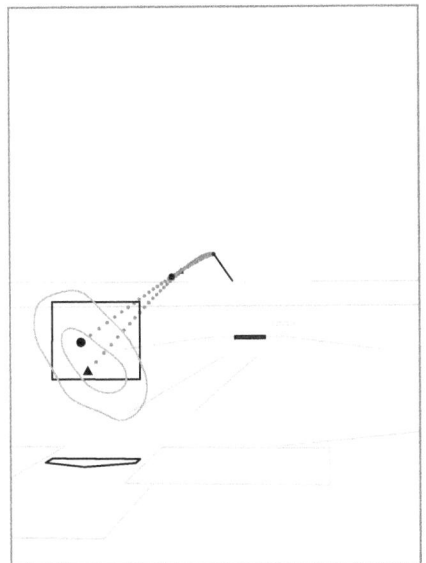

## Pitch Shape vs RHH

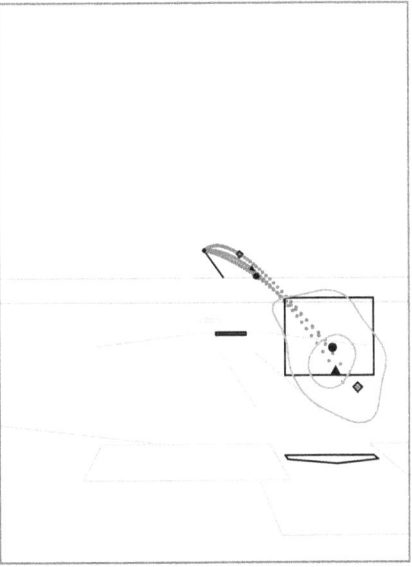

| Type | Frequency | Velocity | H Movement | V Movement |
|---|---|---|---|---|
| ● Fastball | 54.5% | 94.5 [106] | -8.9 [89] | -13.7 [104] |
| ▲ Changeup | 27.3% | 85.3 [101] | -10.5 [107] | -30 [93] |
| ◇ Curveball | 18.0% | 77.8 [97] | 8.2 [103] | -51.8 [92] |

# Cincinnati Reds 2021

## Michael Lorenzen   RHP
Born: 01/04/92   Age: 29   Bats: R   Throws: R
Height: 6'3"   Weight: 217   Origin: Round 1, 2013 Draft (#38 overall)

| YEAR | TEAM | LVL | AGE | W | L | SV | G | GS | IP | H | HR | BB/9 | K/9 | K | GB% | BABIP |
|---|---|---|---|---|---|---|---|---|---|---|---|---|---|---|---|---|
| 2018 | CIN | MLB | 26 | 4 | 2 | 1 | 45 | 3 | 81 | 78 | 6 | 3.8 | 6.0 | 54 | 49.4% | .294 |
| 2019 | CIN | MLB | 27 | 1 | 4 | 7 | 73 | 0 | 83[1] | 68 | 9 | 3.0 | 9.2 | 85 | 44.3% | .274 |
| 2020 | CIN | MLB | 28 | 3 | 1 | 0 | 18 | 2 | 33[2] | 30 | 3 | 4.5 | 9.4 | 35 | 50.0% | .300 |
| 2021 FS | CIN | MLB | 29 | 9 | 8 | 0 | 26 | 26 | 150 | 139 | 19 | 4.0 | 9.1 | 150 | 48.0% | .294 |
| 2021 DC | CIN | MLB | 29 | 9 | 4 | 0 | 65 | 4 | 74.7 | 69 | 9 | 4.0 | 9.1 | 75 | 48.0% | .294 |

Comparables: Drew VerHagen, Kevin McCarthy, Austin Brice

Lorenzen has spent six seasons in Cincinnati, but like a high school football player whose recruitment portfolio lists his position as "Athlete" the Reds are still working through how best to deploy him. He can play a credible center field and knows how to hit but the idea of Mikey Biceps becoming a true two-way player seems to have reached its expiration date. Instead Lorenzen has found success as a multi-inning reliever and spot starter, where his high-octane fastball and three secondaries miss just enough bats to overcome the occasional flurry of walks. Two successful starts down the stretch last year gave Lorenzen hope he can move back into the rotation, but the strapping Californian is best cast as a rubber-armed bullpen security blanket.

| YEAR | TEAM | LVL | AGE | WHIP | ERA | DRA- | WARP | MPH | FB% | WHF | CSP |
|---|---|---|---|---|---|---|---|---|---|---|---|
| 2018 | CIN | MLB | 26 | 1.38 | 3.11 | 131 | -0.8 | 97.2 | 51.5% | 16.6% | |
| 2019 | CIN | MLB | 27 | 1.15 | 2.92 | 77 | 1.4 | 98.4 | 35.8% | 31.0% | |
| 2020 | CIN | MLB | 28 | 1.40 | 4.28 | 85 | 0.6 | 98.9 | 40.5% | 35.5% | |
| 2021 FS | CIN | MLB | 29 | 1.37 | 4.12 | 93 | 2.0 | 98.3 | 40.9% | 29.2% | 43.8% |
| 2021 DC | CIN | MLB | 29 | 1.37 | 4.12 | 93 | 0.7 | 98.3 | 40.9% | 29.2% | 43.8% |

*Michael Lorenzen, continued*

## Pitch Shape vs LHH

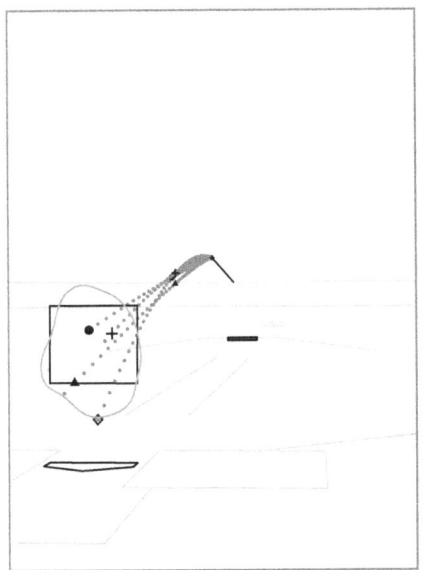

## Pitch Shape vs RHH

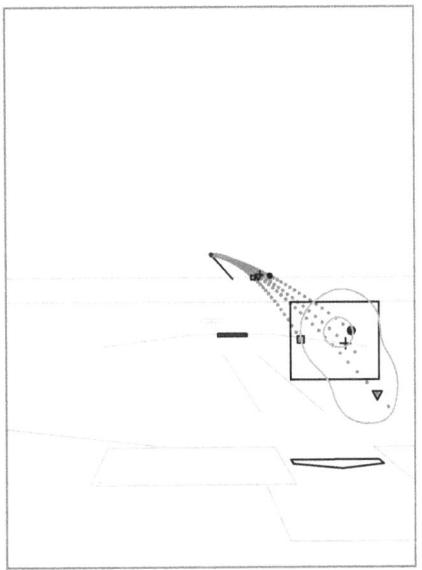

| Type | Frequency | Velocity | H Movement | V Movement |
|---|---|---|---|---|
| ● Fastball | 32.2% | 97.1 [114] | -9.7 [85] | -11.3 [111] |
| ☐ Sinker | 8.0% | 96 [119] | -13.8 [94] | -14.6 [119] |
| + Cutter | 17.6% | 92.9 [129] | -0.2 [86] | -19.5 [119] |
| ▲ Changeup | 17.6% | 86.9 [107] | -14.2 [87] | -23.9 [110] |
| ▽ Slider | 17.0% | 85.2 [106] | 7.9 [110] | -35.1 [96] |
| ◇ Curveball | 6.9% | 82.9 [117] | 4.2 [86] | -48.7 [99] |

# Cincinnati Reds 2021

## Tyler Mahle  RHP

Born: 09/29/94   Age: 26   Bats: R   Throws: R
Height: 6'3"   Weight: 210   Origin: Round 7, 2013 Draft (#225 overall)

| YEAR | TEAM | LVL | AGE | W | L | SV | G | GS | IP | H | HR | BB/9 | K/9 | K | GB% | BABIP |
|---|---|---|---|---|---|---|---|---|---|---|---|---|---|---|---|---|
| 2018 | LOU | AAA | 23 | 2 | 1 | 0 | 5 | 5 | $29^2$ | 22 | 4 | 3.3 | 6.1 | 20 | 37.8% | .212 |
| 2018 | CIN | MLB | 23 | 7 | 9 | 0 | 23 | 23 | 112 | 125 | 22 | 4.3 | 8.8 | 110 | 37.6% | .329 |
| 2019 | LOU | AAA | 24 | 1 | 2 | 0 | 3 | 3 | 9 | 8 | 0 | 3.0 | 13.0 | 13 | 60.0% | .400 |
| 2019 | CIN | MLB | 24 | 3 | 12 | 0 | 25 | 25 | $129^2$ | 136 | 25 | 2.4 | 9.0 | 129 | 47.0% | .308 |
| 2020 | CIN | MLB | 25 | 2 | 2 | 0 | 10 | 9 | $47^2$ | 34 | 6 | 4.0 | 11.3 | 60 | 30.2% | .255 |
| 2021 FS | CIN | MLB | 26 | 9 | 8 | 0 | 26 | 26 | 150 | 138 | 25 | 3.0 | 9.8 | 163 | 39.1% | .293 |
| 2021 DC | CIN | MLB | 26 | 8 | 7 | 0 | 27 | 25 | 129.3 | 119 | 22 | 3.0 | 9.8 | 141 | 39.1% | .293 |

Comparables: Reynaldo López, Jake Faria, Antonio Senzatela

Since arriving in Cincinnati four seasons ago Mahle has continually tinkered with his pitches and his process, and last year something seemed to click. In a series of adjustments best imagined as an up-tempo 80s training montage, Mahle rose before dawn, drank six raw eggs for breakfast, ditched his curve ball and cutter in favor of a new, sharp-breaking slider-cutter hybrid, somehow added significantly more spin to all his pitches and shocked the world. He was suddenly striking out more than a batter per inning, and his new breaker paired so well with the splitter Mahle deploys against lefty bats that he was able to erase his often ghastly platoon splits. Mahle also reverted to his extreme fly-ball tendencies yet managed to keep most of them in the yard, a combination that seems unlikely to continue in Cincinnati's bandbox. Taken together, even with a few more gopher balls thrown in, this latest version of Mahle should thrive in the middle of the rotation.

| YEAR | TEAM | LVL | AGE | WHIP | ERA | DRA- | WARP | MPH | FB% | WHF | CSP |
|---|---|---|---|---|---|---|---|---|---|---|---|
| 2018 | LOU | AAA | 23 | 1.11 | 2.73 | 157 | -0.7 | | | | |
| 2018 | CIN | MLB | 23 | 1.59 | 4.98 | 140 | -1.3 | 95.5 | 67.7% | 24.1% | |
| 2019 | LOU | AAA | 24 | 1.22 | 4.00 | 69 | 0.3 | | | | |
| 2019 | CIN | MLB | 24 | 1.31 | 5.14 | 98 | 1.3 | 95.8 | 56.7% | 23.1% | |
| 2020 | CIN | MLB | 25 | 1.15 | 3.59 | 97 | 0.5 | 96.2 | 55.9% | 33.8% | |
| 2021 FS | CIN | MLB | 26 | 1.25 | 4.04 | 92 | 2.1 | 95.9 | 59.0% | 26.4% | 47.6% |
| 2021 DC | CIN | MLB | 26 | 1.25 | 4.04 | 92 | 1.8 | 95.9 | 59.0% | 26.4% | 47.6% |

**Tyler Mahle, continued**

### Pitch Shape vs LHH

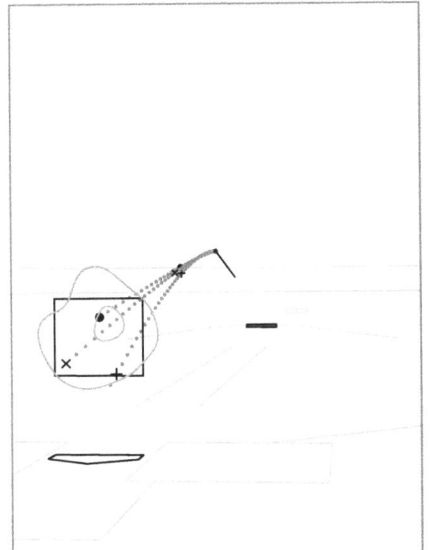

### Pitch Shape vs RHH

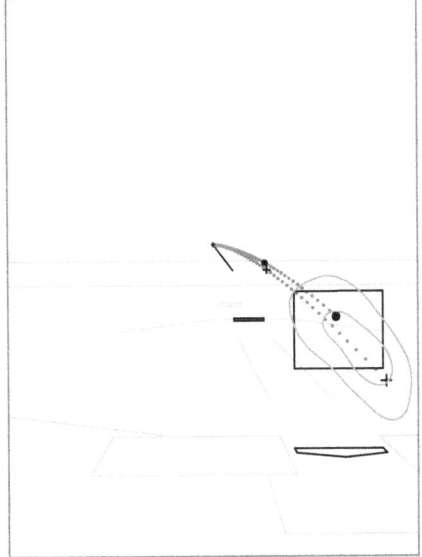

| Type | Frequency | Velocity | H Movement | V Movement |
|---|---|---|---|---|
| ● Fastball | 55.9% | 94.1 [105] | -11 [79] | -12.2 [108] |
| + Cutter | 27.7% | 87.4 [94] | 3.2 [108] | -28.1 [85] |
| × Splitter | 10.8% | 87.5 [110] | -12.4 [83] | -23 [121] |
| ▽ Slider | 5.3% | 85.6 [107] | 3.9 [95] | -35.1 [96] |

# Cincinnati Reds 2021

## Wade Miley  LHP

Born: 11/13/86   Age: 34   Bats: L   Throws: L
Height: 6'2"   Weight: 220   Origin: Round 1, 2008 Draft (#43 overall)

| YEAR | TEAM | LVL | AGE | W | L | SV | G | GS | IP | H | HR | BB/9 | K/9 | K | GB% | BABIP |
|---|---|---|---|---|---|---|---|---|---|---|---|---|---|---|---|---|
| 2018 | BLX | AA | 31 | 1 | 2 | 0 | 7 | 7 | 25$^1$ | 27 | 3 | 1.4 | 9.9 | 28 | 59.4% | .393 |
| 2018 | MIL | MLB | 31 | 5 | 2 | 0 | 16 | 16 | 80$^2$ | 71 | 3 | 3.0 | 5.6 | 50 | 50.4% | .274 |
| 2019 | HOU | MLB | 32 | 14 | 6 | 0 | 33 | 33 | 167$^1$ | 164 | 23 | 3.3 | 7.5 | 140 | 49.1% | .289 |
| 2020 | CIN | MLB | 33 | 0 | 3 | 0 | 6 | 4 | 14$^1$ | 15 | 1 | 5.7 | 7.5 | 12 | 52.3% | .326 |
| 2021 FS | CIN | MLB | 34 | 9 | 9 | 0 | 26 | 26 | 150 | 150 | 22 | 4.1 | 7.5 | 124 | 49.1% | .291 |
| 2021 DC | CIN | MLB | 34 | 7 | 7 | 0 | 24 | 22 | 113.3 | 113 | 17 | 4.1 | 7.5 | 93 | 49.1% | .291 |

Comparables: Homer Bailey, Iván Nova, Tommy Milone

After the Cubs ambushed him for six runs in under two innings during his first Redlegs start, Miley limped off with a groin injury (insert joke here), returned to make three more starts before a bum wing cost him another month and limited him to two mop-up appearances down the stretch. That's not exactly the production Cincinnati hoped for when they signed the low-velo junkballer to solidify the end of their rotation. We all know what Miley is and what he isn't, and it's a coin flip whether his moxie and pitchability can induce enough ground balls to walk the razor's edge one more time.

| YEAR | TEAM | LVL | AGE | WHIP | ERA | DRA- | WARP | MPH | FB% | WHF | CSP |
|---|---|---|---|---|---|---|---|---|---|---|---|
| 2018 | BLX | AA | 31 | 1.22 | 3.55 | 77 | 0.5 | | | | |
| 2018 | MIL | MLB | 31 | 1.21 | 2.57 | 92 | 1.1 | 93.4 | 20.0% | 22.4% | |
| 2019 | HOU | MLB | 32 | 1.34 | 3.98 | 111 | 0.6 | 92.8 | 21.9% | 23.2% | |
| 2020 | CIN | MLB | 33 | 1.67 | 5.65 | 109 | 0.1 | 92.7 | 14.0% | 30.8% | |
| 2021 FS | CIN | MLB | 34 | 1.46 | 4.74 | 105 | 1.1 | 92.9 | 20.7% | 23.9% | 42.3% |
| 2021 DC | CIN | MLB | 34 | 1.46 | 4.74 | 105 | 0.8 | 92.9 | 20.7% | 23.9% | 42.3% |

**Wade Miley, continued**

| Pitch Shape vs LHH | Pitch Shape vs RHH |
|---|---|
| 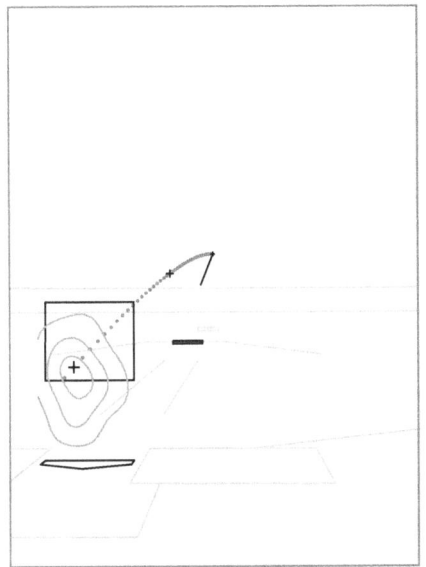 | 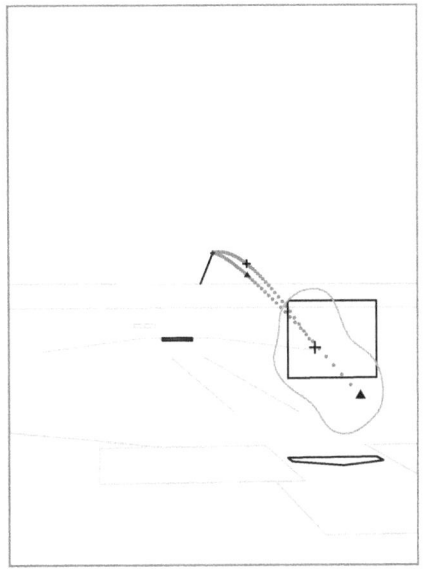 |

| Type | Frequency | Velocity | H Movement | V Movement |
|---|---|---|---|---|
| ● Fastball | 10.2% | 90.5 [93] | 1.4 [125] | -15.7 [99] |
| ☐ Sinker | 3.9% | 89.8 [86] | 10.9 [116] | -18.5 [107] |
| + Cutter | 49.5% | 86.2 [86] | -4.5 [117] | -28.1 [85] |
| ▲ Changeup | 23.5% | 82.4 [89] | 12.8 [94] | -30.2 [93] |
| ◇ Curveball | 10.9% | 75.2 [87] | -8.2 [102] | -54.2 [87] |

## Josh Osich  LHP

Born: 09/03/88  Age: 32  Bats: L  Throws: L
Height: 6'2"  Weight: 235  Origin: Round 6, 2011 Draft (#207 overall)

| YEAR | TEAM | LVL | AGE | W | L | SV | G | GS | IP | H | HR | BB/9 | K/9 | K | GB% | BABIP |
|---|---|---|---|---|---|---|---|---|---|---|---|---|---|---|---|---|
| 2018 | SAC | AAA | 29 | 0 | 0 | 0 | 37 | 2 | 45$^1$ | 56 | 2 | 3.6 | 8.3 | 42 | 44.0% | .370 |
| 2018 | SF | MLB | 29 | 0 | 0 | 0 | 12 | 0 | 12 | 20 | 2 | 5.2 | 7.5 | 10 | 45.2% | .450 |
| 2019 | CHW | MLB | 30 | 4 | 0 | 0 | 57 | 0 | 67$^2$ | 62 | 15 | 2.0 | 8.1 | 61 | 41.3% | .260 |
| 2020 | CIN | MLB | 31 | 1 | 1 | 0 | 17 | 1 | 18$^1$ | 21 | 6 | 2.5 | 11.8 | 24 | 54.5% | .306 |
| 2021 FS | CIN | MLB | 32 | 2 | 2 | 0 | 57 | 0 | 50 | 47 | 7 | 3.5 | 8.9 | 49 | 46.2% | .295 |

Comparables: Hunter Strickland, Heath Hembree, Sam Freeman

Osich was a "trade-deadline addition" in only the strictest definition of the phrase. That the Cubs felt the need to surrender an asset for him served as an indictment of boh the market and the state of Chicago's bullpen. To his credit, he started missing bats at an above-average rate for the first time in his career. His DRA suggested he was better than his ERA, too. Even so, the Cubs mostly stashed him at the alternate site in lieu of giving him serious big-league burn, suggesting even they weren't sold on him being more than a depth piece. Then they designated him for assignment, suggesting it even more strongly.

| YEAR | TEAM | LVL | AGE | WHIP | ERA | DRA- | WARP | MPH | FB% | WHF | CSP |
|---|---|---|---|---|---|---|---|---|---|---|---|
| 2018 | SAC | AAA | 29 | 1.63 | 4.96 | 87 | 0.6 | | | | |
| 2018 | SF | MLB | 29 | 2.25 | 8.25 | 148 | -0.2 | 96.9 | 48.5% | 27.4% | |
| 2019 | CHW | MLB | 30 | 1.14 | 4.66 | 92 | 0.6 | 96.3 | 16.9% | 27.6% | |
| 2020 | CIN | MLB | 31 | 1.42 | 6.38 | 81 | 0.4 | 94.2 | 37.5% | 26.5% | |
| 2021 FS | CIN | MLB | 32 | 1.33 | 4.12 | 95 | 0.4 | 95.7 | 24.9% | 27.3% | 48.8% |

*Josh Osich, continued*

## Pitch Shape vs LHH

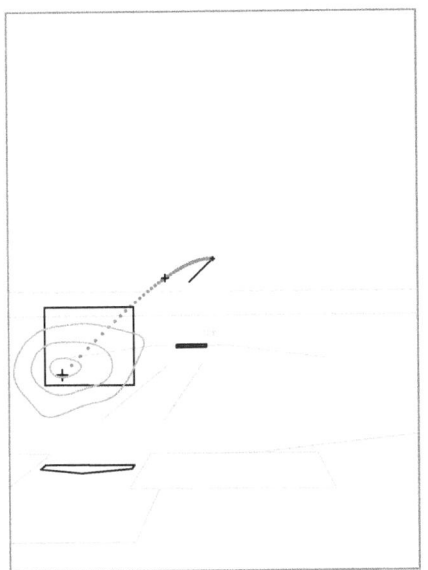

## Pitch Shape vs RHH

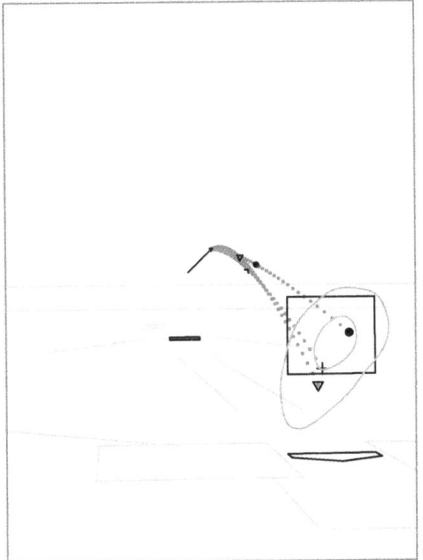

| Type | Frequency | Velocity | H Movement | V Movement |
|---|---|---|---|---|
| ● Fastball | 23.4% | 92.4 [99] | 3 [118] | -20.1 [86] |
| □ Sinker | 14.1% | 92.8 [102] | 10.5 [119] | -22.2 [95] |
| + Cutter | 47.4% | 87.3 [94] | -2.7 [105] | -28.5 [83] |
| ▽ Slider | 15.1% | 77 [69] | -1.4 [86] | -46.5 [63] |

# Cincinnati Reds 2021

## Cionel Pérez  LHP

Born: 04/21/96  Age: 25  Bats: L  Throws: L
Height: 5'11"  Weight: 162  Origin: International Free Agent, 2016

| YEAR | TEAM | LVL | AGE | W | L | SV | G | GS | IP | H | HR | BB/9 | K/9 | K | GB% | BABIP |
|---|---|---|---|---|---|---|---|---|---|---|---|---|---|---|---|---|
| 2018 | CC | AA | 22 | 6 | 1 | 1 | 16 | 11 | $68^1$ | 54 | 3 | 2.9 | 10.9 | 83 | 46.8% | .304 |
| 2018 | FRE | AAA | 22 | 1 | 0 | 0 | 4 | 0 | $5^1$ | 5 | 0 | 10.1 | 10.1 | 6 | 50.0% | .357 |
| 2018 | HOU | MLB | 22 | 0 | 0 | 0 | 8 | 0 | $11^1$ | 6 | 3 | 5.6 | 9.5 | 12 | 57.7% | .130 |
| 2019 | AST | ROK | 23 | 0 | 0 | 0 | 3 | 3 | $5^2$ | 6 | 0 | 4.8 | 22.2 | 14 | 37.5% | .857 |
| 2019 | FAY | HI-A | 23 | 1 | 0 | 0 | 1 | 0 | 2 | 2 | 0 | 0.0 | 4.5 | 1 | 71.4% | .286 |
| 2019 | RR | AAA | 23 | 2 | 1 | 0 | 13 | 10 | 47 | 53 | 6 | 4.6 | 8.2 | 43 | 52.4% | .346 |
| 2019 | HOU | MLB | 23 | 1 | 1 | 0 | 5 | 0 | 9 | 11 | 3 | 2.0 | 7.0 | 7 | 48.4% | .286 |
| 2020 | HOU | MLB | 24 | 0 | 0 | 0 | 7 | 0 | $6^1$ | 7 | 0 | 8.5 | 11.4 | 8 | 61.1% | .389 |
| 2021 FS | CIN | MLB | 25 | 2 | 3 | 0 | 57 | 0 | 50 | 47 | 7 | 5.4 | 9.1 | 50 | 48.4% | .297 |
| 2021 DC | CIN | MLB | 25 | 2 | 2 | 0 | 53 | 0 | 43 | 40 | 6 | 5.4 | 9.1 | 43 | 48.4% | .297 |

Comparables: Yohander Méndez, Justus Sheffield, Ranger Suárez

The decision to leave Pérez off the ALCS roster in favor of Chase De Jong and his 14.73 ERA speaks volumes about how much trust the team is willing to place in the former teenage star. A delayed start to the season didn't help, nor did walking almost a batter per inning in his limited work. Length and command were plainly stated as the reasons for the choice, which is a neat encapsulation of where we're at with Pérez. The stuff still plays on the sporadic occasions he does locate but his innings total keeps dropping every season and there's little evidence he can handle being a multi-inning reliever, let alone start. We have never seen Pérez face even 50 batters in a single major-league season, his options exhausted for little return. Nevertheless, Houston has to make a decision: either place their trust in Pérez as a regular member of their staff or designate him for assignment.

| YEAR | TEAM | LVL | AGE | WHIP | ERA | DRA- | WARP | MPH | FB% | WHF | CSP |
|---|---|---|---|---|---|---|---|---|---|---|---|
| 2018 | CC | AA | 22 | 1.11 | 1.98 | 62 | 1.7 | | | | |
| 2018 | FRE | AAA | 22 | 2.06 | 3.38 | 63 | 0.1 | | | | |
| 2018 | HOU | MLB | 22 | 1.15 | 3.97 | 102 | 0.0 | 96.9 | 63.2% | 26.3% | |
| 2019 | AST | ROK | 23 | 1.59 | 3.18 | | | | | | |
| 2019 | FAY | HI-A | 23 | 1.00 | 0.00 | 88 | 0.0 | | | | |
| 2019 | RR | AAA | 23 | 1.64 | 5.36 | 100 | 0.8 | | | | |
| 2019 | HOU | MLB | 23 | 1.44 | 10.00 | 139 | -0.1 | 97.2 | 61.5% | 23.6% | |
| 2020 | HOU | MLB | 24 | 2.05 | 2.84 | 80 | 0.1 | 96.5 | 62.5% | 31.5% | |
| 2021 FS | CIN | MLB | 25 | 1.55 | 4.89 | 105 | 0.1 | 96.8 | 62.3% | 27.5% | 41.2% |
| 2021 DC | CIN | MLB | 25 | 1.55 | 4.89 | 105 | 0.1 | 96.8 | 62.3% | 27.5% | 41.2% |

*Cionel Pérez, continued*

### Pitch Shape vs LHH

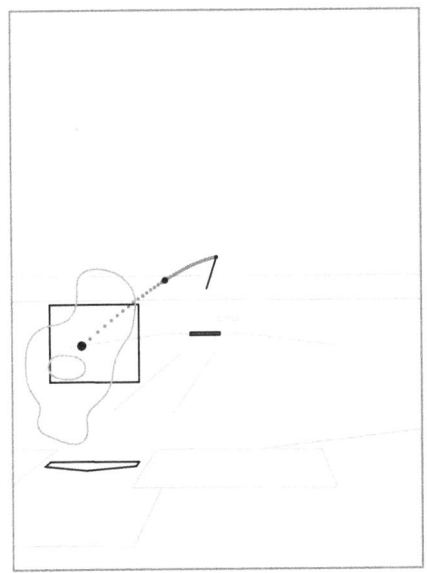

### Pitch Shape vs RHH

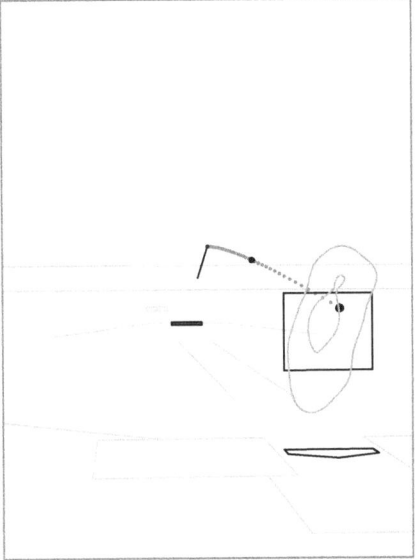

| Type | Frequency | Velocity | H Movement | V Movement |
|---|---|---|---|---|
| ● Fastball | 61.1% | 95.1 [108] | 4.2 [112] | -12.9 [107] |
| ▽ Slider | 33.6% | 83.9 [100] | -10 [118] | -38.8 [85] |

Reds Player Analysis - 63

# Cincinnati Reds 2021

## Noé Ramirez   RHP
Born: 12/22/89   Age: 31   Bats: R   Throws: R
Height: 6'3"   Weight: 205   Origin: Round 4, 2011 Draft (#142 overall)

| YEAR | TEAM | LVL | AGE | W | L | SV | G | GS | IP | H | HR | BB/9 | K/9 | K | GB% | BABIP |
|---|---|---|---|---|---|---|---|---|---|---|---|---|---|---|---|---|
| 2018 | LAA | MLB | 28 | 7 | 5 | 1 | 69 | 1 | 83¹ | 75 | 15 | 3.2 | 10.3 | 95 | 43.7% | .290 |
| 2019 | LAA | MLB | 29 | 5 | 4 | 0 | 51 | 7 | 67² | 59 | 9 | 2.7 | 10.5 | 79 | 38.1% | .299 |
| 2020 | LAA | MLB | 30 | 1 | 0 | 0 | 21 | 0 | 21 | 15 | 2 | 3.9 | 6.0 | 14 | 39.3% | .220 |
| 2021 FS | CIN | MLB | 31 | 2 | 2 | 0 | 57 | 0 | 50 | 47 | 9 | 3.6 | 9.1 | 50 | 39.1% | .287 |
| 2021 DC | CIN | MLB | 31 | 2 | 2 | 0 | 47 | 0 | 49 | 46 | 8 | 3.6 | 9.1 | 49 | 39.1% | .287 |

Comparables: Heath Hembree, Tommy Kahnle, Paul Sewald

In a September postgame appearance answering questions via Zoom, Anthony Rendon had his session crashed by Ramirez, who introduced himself as "your Mexican teammate here" and grilled Rendon on his choice of taco. Rendon gave a quintessentially Texan answer, answering with Steak Fajita (a Californian would say Carne Asada) and quipping, "Y'all put avocado on everything." By that description Ramirez has been the avocado of the Angels bullpen in recent seasons, popping up everywhere (151 innings between 2018-19) and adding a little something despite the continued protests of overuse by detractors. His barely 90 mph velocity is starting to tilt toward almost 90 mph, and the righty last season ceased outpacing his ERA by DRA after his strikeout rate plummeted. Falling out of favor with manager Joe Maddon despite ultimately good traditional stats, Ramirez twice went at least nine days between appearances. Every avocado goes brown a little faster than you think it's going to.

| YEAR | TEAM | LVL | AGE | WHIP | ERA | DRA- | WARP | MPH | FB% | WHF | CSP |
|---|---|---|---|---|---|---|---|---|---|---|---|
| 2018 | LAA | MLB | 28 | 1.26 | 4.54 | 75 | 1.5 | 91.6 | 42.0% | 27.9% | |
| 2019 | LAA | MLB | 29 | 1.17 | 3.99 | 79 | 1.1 | 90.6 | 28.4% | 31.0% | |
| 2020 | LAA | MLB | 30 | 1.14 | 3.00 | 113 | 0.0 | 90.1 | 36.0% | 25.3% | |
| 2021 FS | CIN | MLB | 31 | 1.35 | 4.52 | 100 | 0.2 | 90.8 | 34.1% | 28.8% | 46.2% |
| 2021 DC | CIN | MLB | 31 | 1.35 | 4.52 | 100 | 0.2 | 90.8 | 34.1% | 28.8% | 46.2% |

**Noé Ramirez, continued**

## Pitch Shape vs LHH

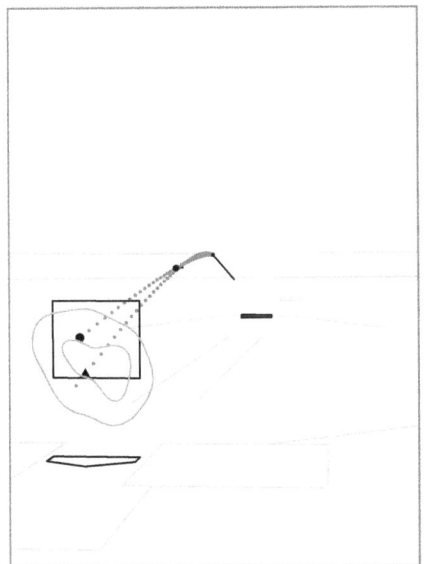

## Pitch Shape vs RHH

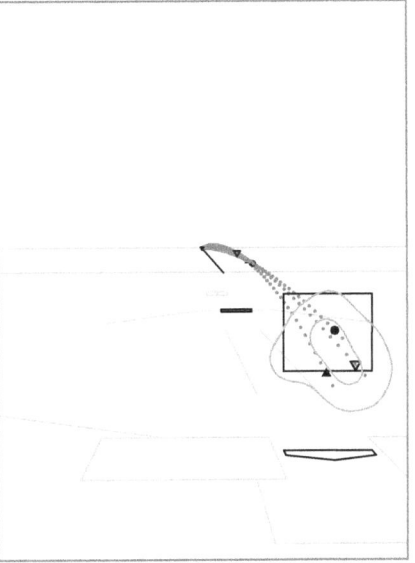

| Type | Frequency | Velocity | H Movement | V Movement |
|---|---|---|---|---|
| ● Fastball | 35.4% | 88.8 [88] | -8.7 [91] | -19.8 [87] |
| ▲ Changeup | 32.5% | 83.5 [94] | -12.1 [98] | -39.8 [66] |
| ▽ Slider | 30.4% | 76.8 [68] | 10.3 [119] | -43.7 [71] |

# Cincinnati Reds 2021

## Lucas Sims  RHP
Born: 05/10/94  Age: 27  Bats: R  Throws: R
Height: 6'2"  Weight: 225  Origin: Round 1, 2012 Draft (#21 overall)

| YEAR | TEAM | LVL | AGE | W | L | SV | G | GS | IP | H | HR | BB/9 | K/9 | K | GB% | BABIP |
|---|---|---|---|---|---|---|---|---|---|---|---|---|---|---|---|---|
| 2018 | GWN | AAA | 24 | 4 | 3 | 0 | 15 | 14 | 73 | 66 | 6 | 4.2 | 10.2 | 83 | 42.6% | .333 |
| 2018 | LOU | AAA | 24 | 0 | 2 | 0 | 5 | 5 | 28$^1$ | 20 | 5 | 1.6 | 10.2 | 32 | 29.2% | .224 |
| 2018 | ATL | MLB | 24 | 0 | 0 | 0 | 6 | 0 | 10$^1$ | 12 | 2 | 7.0 | 8.7 | 10 | 42.4% | .323 |
| 2018 | CIN | MLB | 24 | 0 | 0 | 0 | 3 | 0 | 5$^1$ | 3 | 1 | 8.4 | 10.1 | 6 | 23.1% | .167 |
| 2019 | LOU | AAA | 25 | 5 | 0 | 0 | 16 | 16 | 79 | 69 | 9 | 4.1 | 11.6 | 102 | 31.0% | .324 |
| 2019 | CIN | MLB | 25 | 2 | 1 | 0 | 24 | 4 | 43 | 31 | 8 | 4.0 | 11.9 | 57 | 25.3% | .256 |
| 2020 | CIN | MLB | 26 | 3 | 0 | 0 | 20 | 0 | 25$^2$ | 13 | 3 | 3.9 | 11.9 | 34 | 41.8% | .192 |
| 2021 FS | CIN | MLB | 27 | 2 | 2 | 3 | 57 | 0 | 50 | 42 | 8 | 4.3 | 11.2 | 62 | 35.8% | .290 |
| 2021 DC | CIN | MLB | 27 | 2 | 2 | 3 | 53 | 0 | 49 | 41 | 8 | 4.3 | 11.2 | 61 | 35.8% | .290 |

Comparables: Robert Stephenson, Drew Anderson, Matt Wisler

"Be great at what you're good at" is Cincinnati's new pitching motto, and Sims has taken that to heart and found success in the Reds bullpen. The former Brave ditched his changeup and focused on increasing the spin on his already gyroscopic fastball and breakers, resulting in the debut of his unholy terror of a slurve. It darts under the hands of baffled lefties, plays peek-a-boo with righties and allows Sims to change eye levels by working his four-seamer up in the zone. His command is still fringy and gopher balls will always be a risk, but Sims has developed an arsenal that can work in the late innings.

| YEAR | TEAM | LVL | AGE | WHIP | ERA | DRA- | WARP | MPH | FB% | WHF | CSP |
|---|---|---|---|---|---|---|---|---|---|---|---|
| 2018 | GWN | AAA | 24 | 1.37 | 2.84 | 88 | 1.0 | | | | |
| 2018 | LOU | AAA | 24 | 0.88 | 3.81 | 84 | 0.4 | | | | |
| 2018 | ATL | MLB | 24 | 1.94 | 7.84 | 142 | -0.2 | 94.8 | 55.7% | 24.1% | |
| 2018 | CIN | MLB | 24 | 1.50 | 6.75 | 80 | 0.1 | 94.0 | 55.0% | 34.0% | |
| 2019 | LOU | AAA | 25 | 1.33 | 4.56 | 71 | 2.5 | | | | |
| 2019 | CIN | MLB | 25 | 1.16 | 4.60 | 88 | 0.6 | 95.3 | 50.6% | 34.1% | |
| 2020 | CIN | MLB | 26 | 0.94 | 2.45 | 84 | 0.4 | 95.6 | 48.1% | 35.2% | |
| 2021 FS | CIN | MLB | 27 | 1.32 | 4.21 | 93 | 0.4 | 95.4 | 50.0% | 34.0% | 41.3% |
| 2021 DC | CIN | MLB | 27 | 1.32 | 4.21 | 93 | 0.4 | 95.4 | 50.0% | 34.0% | 41.3% |

**Lucas Sims, continued**

### Pitch Shape vs LHH

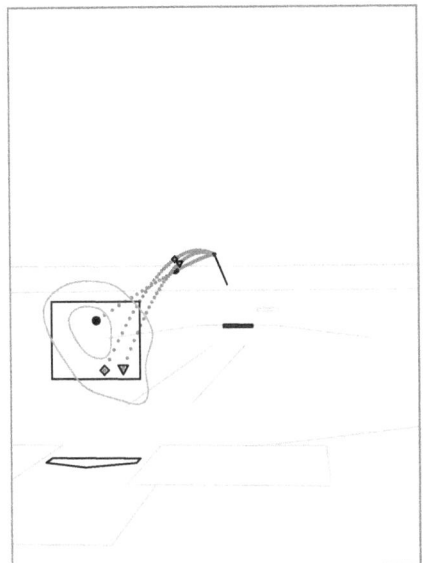

### Pitch Shape vs RHH

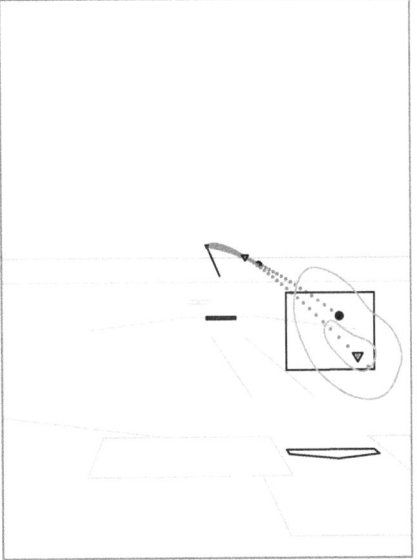

| Type | Frequency | Velocity | H Movement | V Movement |
|---|---|---|---|---|
| ● Fastball | 47.6% | 94.1 [105] | -6.4 [101] | -11.4 [111] |
| ▽ Slider | 33.3% | 82.9 [95] | 12.8 [128] | -37.3 [90] |
| ◇ Curveball | 16.7% | 81.1 [110] | 13.4 [124] | -43.4 [111] |

Cincinnati Reds 2021

## Tyler Thornburg  RHP
Born: 09/29/88  Age: 32  Bats: R  Throws: R
Height: 5'11"  Weight: 190  Origin: Round 3, 2010 Draft (#96 overall)

| YEAR | TEAM | LVL | AGE | W | L | SV | G | GS | IP | H | HR | BB/9 | K/9 | K | GB% | BABIP |
|---|---|---|---|---|---|---|---|---|---|---|---|---|---|---|---|---|
| 2018 | WOR | AAA | 29 | 0 | 1 | 0 | 15 | 1 | 12$^2$ | 11 | 3 | 4.3 | 7.8 | 11 | 20.0% | .216 |
| 2018 | BOS | MLB | 29 | 2 | 0 | 0 | 25 | 0 | 24 | 28 | 6 | 3.8 | 7.9 | 21 | 37.3% | .319 |
| 2019 | OKC | AAA | 30 | 0 | 0 | 0 | 12 | 0 | 12 | 11 | 3 | 6.8 | 11.2 | 15 | 22.6% | .286 |
| 2019 | WOR | AAA | 30 | 0 | 2 | 0 | 11 | 1 | 10$^2$ | 17 | 5 | 7.6 | 11.0 | 13 | 23.7% | .364 |
| 2019 | BOS | MLB | 30 | 0 | 0 | 0 | 16 | 0 | 18$^2$ | 21 | 4 | 4.8 | 10.6 | 22 | 30.2% | .347 |
| 2020 | CIN | MLB | 31 | 0 | 0 | 0 | 7 | 0 | 7 | 6 | 0 | 6.4 | 12.9 | 10 | 23.5% | .353 |
| 2021 FS | CIN | MLB | 32 | 2 | 3 | 0 | 57 | 0 | 50 | 47 | 10 | 4.6 | 9.5 | 52 | 31.4% | .282 |

Comparables: Alex Colomé, Anthony Bass, Justin Grimm

    Thornburg worked his way back from thoracic outlet surgery to post seven promising innings in the Cincinnati bullpen before breaking down again; he'll spend all of 2021 getting acquainted with the new ligament in his elbow.

| YEAR | TEAM | LVL | AGE | WHIP | ERA | DRA- | WARP | MPH | FB% | WHF | CSP |
|---|---|---|---|---|---|---|---|---|---|---|---|
| 2018 | WOR | AAA | 29 | 1.34 | 4.26 | 120 | -0.1 | | | | |
| 2018 | BOS | MLB | 29 | 1.58 | 5.62 | 111 | 0.0 | 94.4 | 55.6% | 20.9% | |
| 2019 | OKC | AAA | 30 | 1.67 | 6.00 | 81 | 0.3 | | | | |
| 2019 | WOR | AAA | 30 | 2.44 | 12.66 | 175 | -0.2 | | | | |
| 2019 | BOS | MLB | 30 | 1.66 | 7.71 | 133 | -0.2 | 95.1 | 55.0% | 20.9% | |
| 2020 | CIN | MLB | 31 | 1.57 | 3.86 | 91 | 0.1 | 94.8 | 57.2% | 32.2% | |
| 2021 FS | CIN | MLB | 32 | 1.45 | 5.15 | 111 | -0.1 | 94.8 | 55.7% | 23.9% | 45.0% |

*Tyler Thornburg, continued*

## Pitch Shape vs LHH

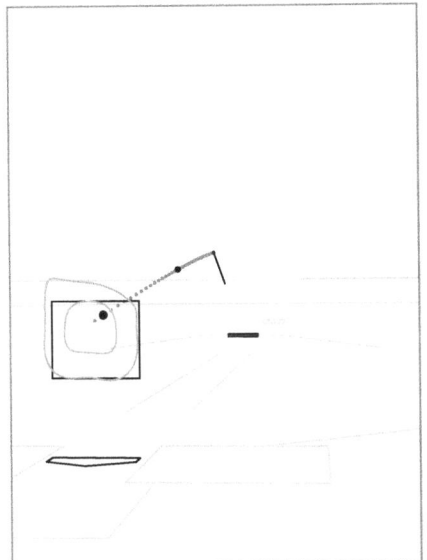

## Pitch Shape vs RHH

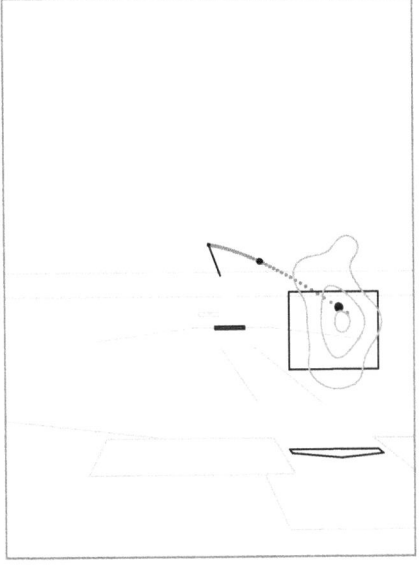

| Type | Frequency | Velocity | H Movement | V Movement |
|---|---|---|---|---|
| ● Fastball | 57.2% | 93.4 [103] | -6.5 [101] | -9.7 [116] |
| ▲ Changeup | 20.7% | 84.1 [96] | -9.5 [112] | -25.3 [106] |
| ◇ Curveball | 22.1% | 76.9 [93] | 8.9 [105] | -55.8 [83] |

# PLAYER COMMENTS WITHOUT GRAPHS

### Wladimir Balentien  LF
Born: 07/02/84   Age: 37   Bats: R   Throws: R
Height: 6'2"   Weight: 220   Origin:

| YEAR | TEAM | LVL | AGE | PA | R | 2B | 3B | HR | RBI | BB | K | SB | CS | AVG/OBP/SLG |
|---|---|---|---|---|---|---|---|---|---|---|---|---|---|---|
| 2018 | YKL | NPB | 33 | 602 | 72 | 22 | 0 | 38 | 131 | 85 | 121 | 1 | 1 | .268/.370/.533 |
| 2019 | YKL | NPB | 34 | 468 | 65 | 13 | 0 | 33 | 93 | 54 | 117 | 0 | 1 | .280/.363/.554 |
| 2020 | FKU | NPB | 35 | 218 | 16 | 7 | 0 | 9 | 22 | 25 | 59 | 0 | 1 | .167/.261/.346 |
| 2021 | | | | | | | | No projection | | | | | | |

Presumably, more than a fair share of scouting reports on Balentien from the early-to-mid 2000s mentioned his enormous raw power. The particularly prescient among them even insisted he would go on to have a lengthy career in Asia if things didn't click for him stateside. It's hard to imagine, however, anyone envisioning him unleashing 60 dingers to break Sadaharu Oh's sacred single-season NPB home run record in 2013, which happened a year after having his own AZL seasonal home run record broken. As of the end of the 2020 campaign, the Curaçao naitive ranks 43rd on the NPB all-time leaderboard with 297 long balls, despite playing roughly half the games of his closest peers. He has been in Japan for so long that in one sense, he has become Japanese; he can be on the roster without occupying one of his team's foreign player spots. On the flip side of the coin, time has crept up on him. It's been quite a run, but there's a good chance Balentien won't play beyond 2021 after his current two-year contract expires.

| YEAR | TEAM | LVL | AGE | PA | DRC+ | BABIP | BRR | FRAA | WARP |
|---|---|---|---|---|---|---|---|---|---|
| 2018 | YKL | NPB | 33 | 602 | | | | | |
| 2019 | YKL | NPB | 34 | 468 | | | | | |
| 2020 | FKU | NPB | 35 | 218 | | | | | |
| 2021 | | | | | | No projection | | | |

## Tucker Barnhart C
Born: 01/07/91   Age: 30   Bats: L   Throws: R
Height: 5'11"   Weight: 192   Origin: Round 10, 2009 Draft (#299 overall)

| YEAR | TEAM | LVL | AGE | PA | R | 2B | 3B | HR | RBI | BB | K | SB | CS | AVG/OBP/SLG |
|---|---|---|---|---|---|---|---|---|---|---|---|---|---|---|
| 2018 | CIN | MLB | 27 | 522 | 50 | 21 | 3 | 10 | 46 | 54 | 96 | 0 | 4 | .248/.328/.372 |
| 2019 | CIN | MLB | 28 | 364 | 32 | 14 | 0 | 11 | 40 | 44 | 83 | 1 | 0 | .231/.328/.380 |
| 2020 | CIN | MLB | 29 | 110 | 10 | 3 | 0 | 5 | 13 | 12 | 28 | 0 | 0 | .204/.291/.388 |
| 2021 FS | CIN | MLB | 30 | 600 | 71 | 23 | 1 | 18 | 66 | 64 | 133 | 2 | 2 | .229/.318/.381 |
| 2021 DC | CIN | MLB | 30 | 342 | 40 | 13 | 0 | 10 | 38 | 36 | 76 | 1 | 1 | .229/.318/.381 |

Comparables: Vic Correll, Mike Fitzgerald, Keith Osik

| YEAR | TEAM | P. COUNT | FRM RUNS | BLK RUNS | THRW RUNS | TOT RUNS |
|---|---|---|---|---|---|---|
| 2018 | CIN | 17031 | -11.5 | 3.6 | -0.3 | -8.1 |
| 2019 | CIN | 13047 | 10.1 | 4.9 | -0.3 | 14.8 |
| 2020 | CIN | 4801 | 2.4 | 0.8 | -0.4 | 2.8 |
| 2021 | CIN | 13228 | -0.2 | 3.8 | 1.3 | 5.0 |
| 2021 | CIN | 13228 | -0.2 | 2.4 | 1.3 | 3.5 |

Metallic-hued hand coverings are once again the hottest item in the Tucker Barnhart catalog, as the veteran receiver earned his second Gold Glove award and the first ever to be determined entirely by defensive metrics. (Ed. note: We've come a long way, baby.) Barnhart's framing has improved over the years and he did an excellent job controlling the running game last summer, which combined with his always-solid blocking and receiving skills to make him a worthy recipient. At the plate, Barnhart gave up switch-hitting and batted exclusively from the left side yet still produced his usual slightly-below-average offensive numbers. That precipitated a virtual job-share with the slightly more potent bat of Curt Casali, as the Reds continued to try anything to shake their lineup out of the doldrums. Barnhart has one guaranteed year left on his current deal, and it will be interesting to see if his defense is valued enough for his $7.5 million option to be picked up.

| YEAR | TEAM | LVL | AGE | PA | DRC+ | BABIP | BRR | FRAA | WARP |
|---|---|---|---|---|---|---|---|---|---|
| 2018 | CIN | MLB | 27 | 522 | 85 | .291 | -3.3 | C(118): -9.6, 1B(11): -0.7 | 0.2 |
| 2019 | CIN | MLB | 28 | 364 | 89 | .278 | -3.7 | C(102): 15.3, 1B(3): 0.0 | 2.5 |
| 2020 | CIN | MLB | 29 | 110 | 91 | .231 | -0.5 | C(36): -0.2, 1B(2): 0.0 | 0.5 |
| 2021 FS | CIN | MLB | 30 | 600 | 89 | .274 | -0.6 | C 7, 1B 0 | 2.2 |
| 2021 DC | CIN | MLB | 30 | 342 | 89 | .274 | -0.4 | C 5 | 1.4 |

# Cincinnati Reds 2021

## Alex Blandino 2B
Born: 11/06/92　Age: 28　Bats: R　Throws: R
Height: 6'0"　Weight: 190　Origin: Round 1, 2014 Draft (#29 overall)

| YEAR | TEAM | LVL | AGE | PA | R | 2B | 3B | HR | RBI | BB | K | SB | CS | AVG/OBP/SLG |
|---|---|---|---|---|---|---|---|---|---|---|---|---|---|---|
| 2018 | CIN | MLB | 25 | 147 | 14 | 4 | 0 | 1 | 8 | 13 | 41 | 0 | 0 | .234/.324/.289 |
| 2019 | LOU | AAA | 26 | 293 | 36 | 13 | 1 | 5 | 24 | 40 | 73 | 1 | 3 | .247/.386/.372 |
| 2019 | CIN | MLB | 26 | 50 | 6 | 1 | 0 | 1 | 3 | 10 | 14 | 0 | 0 | .250/.420/.361 |
| 2021 FS | CIN | MLB | 28 | 600 | 79 | 21 | 1 | 17 | 52 | 69 | 172 | 3 | 2 | .212/.323/.360 |
| 2021 DC | CIN | MLB | 28 | 142 | 18 | 5 | 0 | 4 | 12 | 16 | 40 | 0 | 1 | .212/.323/.360 |

Comparables: Drew Sutton, Colin Walsh, Max Moroff

 Blandino is a product of Silicon Valley and was once a well-regarded start-up. Yet seven years after being drafted in the first round out of Stanford he has yet to become a permanent feature of the MLB platform. Blandino has a solid batting eye, draws walks and slaps singles, but lacks the range, arm and athleticism for shortstop and the power to be a real asset anywhere else. His is a hard skill set to monetize, though he may be able to eventually eke out his pension in a utility role.

| YEAR | TEAM | LVL | AGE | PA | DRC+ | BABIP | BRR | FRAA | WARP |
|---|---|---|---|---|---|---|---|---|---|
| 2018 | CIN | MLB | 25 | 147 | 79 | .337 | 2.3 | 2B(21): -1.4, 3B(15): -1.2, SS(11): -0.8 | 0.0 |
| 2019 | LOU | AAA | 26 | 293 | 108 | .335 | -3.2 | 2B(35): -1.6, SS(18): -1.1, 3B(15): 0.8 | 0.8 |
| 2019 | CIN | MLB | 26 | 50 | 90 | .348 | -0.3 | 2B(10): 0.1, 3B(4): -0.0, 1B(3): -0.0 | 0.1 |
| 2021 FS | CIN | MLB | 28 | 600 | 90 | .281 | -0.6 | SS 0, 2B -2 | 0.6 |
| 2021 DC | CIN | MLB | 28 | 142 | 90 | .281 | -0.1 | SS 0, 2B 0 | 0.2 |

## Tyler Callihan 2B
Born: 06/22/00　Age: 21　Bats: L　Throws: R
Height: 6'1"　Weight: 205　Origin: Round 3, 2019 Draft (#85 overall)

| YEAR | TEAM | LVL | AGE | PA | R | 2B | 3B | HR | RBI | BB | K | SB | CS | AVG/OBP/SLG |
|---|---|---|---|---|---|---|---|---|---|---|---|---|---|---|
| 2019 | GRN | ROK+ | 19 | 217 | 27 | 10 | 5 | 5 | 26 | 9 | 46 | 9 | 3 | .260/.297/.439 |
| 2019 | BIL | ROK+ | 19 | 21 | 3 | 0 | 1 | 1 | 7 | 1 | 4 | 2 | 0 | .400/.429/.650 |
| 2021 FS | CIN | MLB | 21 | 600 | 43 | 19 | 5 | 8 | 49 | 28 | 195 | 16 | 5 | .190/.233/.291 |

 Losing a developmental year is hard on every minor leaguer but especially an older prep prospect like Callihan, who already has less time than most to determine which infield position his iffy glove can handle and prove his power bat can play there.

| YEAR | TEAM | LVL | AGE | PA | DRC+ | BABIP | BRR | FRAA | WARP |
|---|---|---|---|---|---|---|---|---|---|
| 2019 | GRN | ROK+ | 19 | 217 | | .313 | | | |
| 2019 | BIL | ROK+ | 19 | 21 | | .467 | | | |
| 2021 FS | CIN | MLB | 21 | 600 | 41 | .273 | 2.3 | | -2.5 |

## Matt Davidson  1B

Born: 03/26/91   Age: 30   Bats: R   Throws: R
Height: 6'3"   Weight: 230   Origin: Round 1, 2009 Draft (#35 overall)

| YEAR | TEAM | LVL | AGE | PA | R | 2B | 3B | HR | RBI | BB | K | SB | CS | AVG/OBP/SLG |
|---|---|---|---|---|---|---|---|---|---|---|---|---|---|---|
| 2018 | CHW | MLB | 27 | 496 | 51 | 23 | 0 | 20 | 62 | 52 | 165 | 0 | 0 | .228/.319/.419 |
| 2019 | NAS | AAA | 28 | 528 | 74 | 24 | 0 | 33 | 101 | 42 | 151 | 1 | 0 | .264/.339/.527 |
| 2020 | CIN | MLB | 29 | 47 | 3 | 1 | 0 | 3 | 11 | 4 | 13 | 0 | 0 | .163/.234/.395 |
| 2021 FS | CIN | MLB | 30 | 600 | 67 | 20 | 1 | 26 | 76 | 50 | 212 | 0 | 1 | .206/.287/.395 |

Comparables: Dave Kingman, Jeff Liefer, Craig Wilson

Davidson parlayed the 33 minor league dingers he blasted in 2019 into a spring training non-roster invite, and when COVID-19 changed the rules of the game, guess who became the first home designated hitter in Reds history? Davidson popped out weakly, then bounced into a 6-4-3, and things went downhill from there—consider that he only managed one more hit against right-handed pitching than you did last year. On the plus side, the would-be two-way player was able to toss three more blowout innings and showcase his glorious, looping, time-bending curveball, even freezing Mike Freeman with it for a backwards K. Previous talk of Davidson getting a real shot at a bullpen job never seemed to go anywhere, which from an aesthetic standpoint is a real shame. What does anyone have to lose?

| YEAR | TEAM | LVL | AGE | PA | DRC+ | BABIP | BRR | FRAA | WARP |
|---|---|---|---|---|---|---|---|---|---|
| 2018 | CHW | MLB | 27 | 496 | 101 | .313 | -3.9 | 1B(45): -3.1, 3B(14): 0.9, P(3): 0.1 | 0.3 |
| 2019 | NAS | AAA | 28 | 528 | 111 | .315 | -2.6 | 1B(70): -5.1, 3B(27): -0.2, P(1): 0.1 | 1.0 |
| 2020 | CIN | MLB | 29 | 47 | 96 | .148 | -0.2 | P(3): -0.0, 1B(2): 0.1 | 0.1 |
| 2021 FS | CIN | MLB | 30 | 600 | 81 | .284 | -0.9 | 1B -3, 3B 1 | -0.9 |

## Austin Hendrick  CF

Born: 06/15/01   Age: 20   Bats: L   Throws: L
Height: 6'0"   Weight: 195   Origin: Round 1, 2020 Draft (#12 overall)

The Reds nabbed Hendrick with their first pack in last summer's draft and are now impatiently awaiting the day they can unleash his lefty swing on professional pitching in game situations. The Pennsylvania prep product has plus raw power and electrifying bat speed, whipping through the zone to attack pitches and launch towering shots to the right field alley. There will probably be a lot of swing-and-miss in his game, but when he makes contact it has That Sound. There's plenty of work to do, but Hendrick has the arm, athleticism and thunder of a prototypical right fielder and potential home run champ.

# Cincinnati Reds 2021

## Rece Hinds  SS
Born: 09/05/00  Age: 20  Bats: R  Throws: R
Height: 6'4"  Weight: 215  Origin: Round 2, 2019 Draft (#49 overall)

| YEAR | TEAM | LVL | AGE | PA | R | 2B | 3B | HR | RBI | BB | K | SB | CS | AVG/OBP/SLG |
|---|---|---|---|---|---|---|---|---|---|---|---|---|---|---|
| 2019 | GRN | ROK+ | 18 | 10 | 1 | 0 | 0 | 0 | 1 | 2 | 3 | 0 | 0 | .000/.286/.000 |
| 2021 FS | CIN | MLB | 20 | 600 | 43 | 18 | 2 | 8 | 47 | 35 | 228 | | | .176/.231/.267 |

Hinds has only played three professional games since the Reds chose him in the second round of the 2019 draft, but was able to show off his immense raw power and plus makeup as the youngest player at the club's alternate training site; he may not stick at the hot corner, but the juice in his bat just might be an asset anywhere.

| YEAR | TEAM | LVL | AGE | PA | DRC+ | BABIP | BRR | FRAA | WARP |
|---|---|---|---|---|---|---|---|---|---|
| 2019 | GRN | ROK+ | 18 | 10 | | .000 | | | |
| 2021 FS | CIN | MLB | 20 | 600 | 37 | .279 | | | -3.1 |

## Jonathan India  3B
Born: 12/15/96  Age: 24  Bats: R  Throws: R
Height: 6'0"  Weight: 200  Origin: Round 1, 2018 Draft (#5 overall)

| YEAR | TEAM | LVL | AGE | PA | R | 2B | 3B | HR | RBI | BB | K | SB | CS | AVG/OBP/SLG |
|---|---|---|---|---|---|---|---|---|---|---|---|---|---|---|
| 2018 | BIL | ROK | 21 | 10 | 1 | 0 | 0 | 0 | 0 | 0 | 4 | 0 | 1 | .250/.400/.250 |
| 2018 | GRN | ROK | 21 | 62 | 11 | 2 | 1 | 3 | 12 | 15 | 12 | 1 | 0 | .261/.452/.543 |
| 2018 | DAY | LO-A | 21 | 112 | 17 | 7 | 0 | 3 | 11 | 13 | 28 | 5 | 0 | .229/.339/.396 |
| 2019 | DAY | HI-A | 22 | 367 | 50 | 15 | 5 | 8 | 30 | 37 | 84 | 7 | 5 | .256/.346/.410 |
| 2019 | CHA | AA | 22 | 145 | 24 | 3 | 0 | 3 | 14 | 22 | 26 | 4 | 0 | .270/.414/.378 |
| 2021 FS | CIN | MLB | 24 | 600 | 70 | 21 | 3 | 16 | 63 | 62 | 182 | 2 | 2 | .210/.308/.357 |
| 2021 DC | CIN | MLB | 24 | 67 | 7 | 2 | 0 | 1 | 7 | 6 | 20 | 0 | 0 | .210/.308/.357 |

Comparables: Kyle Kubitza, Kelvin Gutierrez, Ty France

Instead of doom-scrolling, raiding the fridge and posting self-righteous jeremiads on social media like the rest of us, India used his COVID summer productively. A good defensive third baseman, the former top draft pick spent his time at Cincinnati's alternate camp working out at second base, increasing his versatility and earning a shot to play a position where his solid-if-uninspiring bat could shine rather than merely survive. India has a disciplined approach and makes hard contact, but hasn't shown the power you would ideally want to see from a third sacker. If he can hack the keystone every day it would raise his ceiling considerably; if not he is unlikely to be more than a fringe-average starter at the hot corner.

| YEAR | TEAM | LVL | AGE | PA | DRC+ | BABIP | BRR | FRAA | WARP |
|---|---|---|---|---|---|---|---|---|---|
| 2018 | BIL | ROK | 21 | 10 | | .500 | | | |
| 2018 | GRN | ROK | 21 | 62 | | .290 | | | |
| 2018 | DAY | LO-A | 21 | 112 | 103 | .292 | 1.5 | 3B(21): 2.4, SS(4): -0.1 | 0.6 |
| 2019 | DAY | HI-A | 22 | 367 | 129 | .319 | -1.8 | 3B(74): -9.2, 2B(5): 0.0 | 1.0 |
| 2019 | CHA | AA | 22 | 145 | 141 | .314 | 0.2 | 3B(33): -0.4 | 1.1 |
| 2021 FS | CIN | MLB | 24 | 600 | 85 | .287 | -0.2 | 3B -3, 2B 0 | -0.2 |
| 2021 DC | CIN | MLB | 24 | 67 | 85 | .287 | 0.0 | 3B 0 | 0.0 |

## Travis Jankowski  RF

Born: 06/15/91   Age: 30   Bats: L   Throws: R
Height: 6'2"   Weight: 190   Origin: Round 1, 2012 Draft (#44 overall)

| YEAR | TEAM | LVL | AGE | PA | R | 2B | 3B | HR | RBI | BB | K | SB | CS | AVG/OBP/SLG |
|---|---|---|---|---|---|---|---|---|---|---|---|---|---|---|
| 2018 | ELP | AAA | 27 | 94 | 17 | 4 | 0 | 1 | 11 | 11 | 21 | 4 | 3 | .362/.452/.450 |
| 2018 | SD | MLB | 27 | 387 | 45 | 12 | 3 | 4 | 17 | 37 | 73 | 24 | 7 | .259/.332/.346 |
| 2019 | ELP | AAA | 28 | 183 | 27 | 6 | 0 | 0 | 12 | 21 | 32 | 7 | 2 | .312/.393/.350 |
| 2019 | SD | MLB | 28 | 24 | 4 | 0 | 0 | 0 | 0 | 2 | 4 | 2 | 2 | .182/.250/.182 |
| 2020 | CIN | MLB | 29 | 17 | 3 | 0 | 0 | 0 | 0 | 2 | 7 | 2 | 1 | .067/.176/.067 |
| 2021 FS | CIN | MLB | 30 | 600 | 54 | 18 | 2 | 8 | 51 | 62 | 159 | 25 | 9 | .221/.308/.311 |

Comparables: Carroll Hardy, Cameron Maybin, Ryan Christenson

A fleet outfielder, Jankowski has by far the most stolen bases (64) of any Jankowski in major league history, needing just nine more to edge out Travis Fryman for the all-time Travis lead. We'll say he's second on the list for players with the middle name Paul because we bet you can't look that up.

| YEAR | TEAM | LVL | AGE | PA | DRC+ | BABIP | BRR | FRAA | WARP |
|---|---|---|---|---|---|---|---|---|---|
| 2018 | ELP | AAA | 27 | 94 | 113 | .483 | 1.5 | CF(20): 2.5 | 0.7 |
| 2018 | SD | MLB | 27 | 387 | 78 | .319 | 4.5 | RF(58): 3.3, CF(34): -1.7, LF(32): -2.2 | 0.4 |
| 2019 | ELP | AAA | 28 | 183 | 91 | .388 | 0.8 | CF(19): -2.2, RF(10): -0.5, LF(8): 0.6 | 0.2 |
| 2019 | SD | MLB | 28 | 24 | 77 | .222 | 0.7 | CF(5): 0.5, RF(5): -0.1, LF(2): -0.1 | 0.1 |
| 2020 | CIN | MLB | 29 | 17 | 71 | .125 | 0.2 | CF(9): 0.2, RF(3): -0.0, LF(1): -0.0 | 0.0 |
| 2021 FS | CIN | MLB | 30 | 600 | 73 | .299 | 1.8 | CF 2, RF 3 | 0.1 |

# Cincinnati Reds 2021

## Mark Payton  LF
Born: 12/07/91   Age: 29   Bats: L   Throws: L
Height: 5'8"   Weight: 180   Origin: Round 7, 2014 Draft (#212 overall)

| YEAR | TEAM | LVL | AGE | PA | R | 2B | 3B | HR | RBI | BB | K | SB | CS | AVG/OBP/SLG |
|---|---|---|---|---|---|---|---|---|---|---|---|---|---|---|
| 2018 | SWB | AAA | 26 | 237 | 29 | 6 | 2 | 6 | 25 | 34 | 49 | 2 | 6 | .259/.368/.401 |
| 2019 | LV | AAA | 27 | 447 | 80 | 30 | 3 | 30 | 97 | 45 | 76 | 7 | 4 | .334/.400/.653 |
| 2020 | CIN | MLB | 28 | 20 | 0 | 1 | 0 | 0 | 0 | 2 | 5 | 1 | 0 | .167/.250/.222 |
| 2021 FS | CIN | MLB | 29 | 600 | 71 | 25 | 2 | 23 | 76 | 51 | 150 | 1 | 1 | .239/.312/.422 |
| 2021 DC | CIN | MLB | 29 | 255 | 30 | 10 | 1 | 9 | 32 | 21 | 64 | 0 | 1 | .239/.312/.422 |

Comparables: Gabe Gross, Alejandro De Aza, Chris Aguila

Via the Rule 5 draft and an eventual trade, Payton parlayed the 30 bombs he hit in 2019—nearly matching his five-year minor league career total—into a big-league roster spot. That power surge happened in Vegas and will stay in Vegas, but Payton has the lefty bat, wheels and glove of a potential reserve outfielder.

| YEAR | TEAM | LVL | AGE | PA | DRC+ | BABIP | BRR | FRAA | WARP |
|---|---|---|---|---|---|---|---|---|---|
| 2018 | SWB | AAA | 26 | 237 | 121 | .312 | -0.1 | LF(40): -0.1, CF(12): -0.1, RF(3): 0.1 | 0.8 |
| 2019 | LV | AAA | 27 | 447 | 138 | .348 | 0.6 | LF(64): 6.1, RF(43): -0.2, CF(5): 0.7 | 3.7 |
| 2020 | CIN | MLB | 28 | 20 | 88 | .231 | | LF(6): -0.1 | 0.0 |
| 2021 FS | CIN | MLB | 29 | 600 | 96 | .292 | -0.6 | LF 4, RF 0 | 1.6 |
| 2021 DC | CIN | MLB | 29 | 255 | 96 | .292 | -0.3 | LF 2, RF 0 | 0.7 |

## Leonardo Rivas  SS
Born: 10/10/97   Age: 23   Bats: S   Throws: R
Height: 5'10"   Weight: 150   Origin: International Free Agent, 2014

| YEAR | TEAM | LVL | AGE | PA | R | 2B | 3B | HR | RBI | BB | K | SB | CS | AVG/OBP/SLG |
|---|---|---|---|---|---|---|---|---|---|---|---|---|---|---|
| 2018 | BUR | LO-A | 20 | 547 | 62 | 16 | 7 | 4 | 34 | 84 | 138 | 16 | 10 | .233/.355/.326 |
| 2019 | ANG | ROK | 21 | 25 | 6 | 0 | 0 | 0 | 8 | 4 | 1 | 0 | | .062/.375/.062 |
| 2019 | IE | HI-A | 21 | 338 | 44 | 14 | 5 | 6 | 26 | 39 | 90 | 4 | 2 | .236/.328/.377 |
| 2021 FS | CIN | MLB | 23 | 600 | 54 | 22 | 3 | 9 | 52 | 66 | 188 | 11 | 6 | .206/.302/.314 |

Comparables: Jorge Mateo, Junior Lake, Manny Machado

Ever noticed that whenever someone says a player is "listed at" a certain height, it carries the implication the height in question is ... in question? Anyway, Rivas is "listed at" five-foot-ten. Sure, he hits with all the force of a ping pong ball in place of a cue ball, but if he can crouch his way to double-digit walks in the upper levels, it could boost him to a major-league utility role. There no one would have impetus to doubt the listed height—as long as he stays away from Aaron Judge in view of photographers.

| YEAR | TEAM | LVL | AGE | PA | DRC+ | BABIP | BRR | FRAA | WARP |
|------|------|-----|-----|-----|------|-------|-----|------|------|
| 2018 | BUR | LO-A | 20 | 547 | 106 | .325 | -0.3 | SS(92): 4.6, 2B(26): 1.1 | 2.4 |
| 2019 | ANG | ROK | 21 | 25 | | .083 | | | |
| 2019 | IE | HI-A | 21 | 338 | 100 | .318 | 0.3 | SS(46): 1.0, 2B(9): -0.7, CF(9): 0.4 | 1.3 |
| 2021 FS | CIN | MLB | 23 | 600 | 72 | .301 | 0.8 | SS 1, 2B 0 | -0.1 |

## Max Schrock  2B

Born: 10/12/94  Age: 26  Bats: L  Throws: R
Height: 5'9"  Weight: 185  Origin: Round 13, 2015 Draft (#404 overall)

| YEAR | TEAM | LVL | AGE | PA | R | 2B | 3B | HR | RBI | BB | K | SB | CS | AVG/OBP/SLG |
|------|------|-----|-----|-----|----|----|----|----|-----|----|----|----|----|-------------|
| 2018 | MEM | AAA | 23 | 457 | 41 | 22 | 0 | 4 | 42 | 24 | 36 | 10 | 5 | .249/.296/.331 |
| 2019 | MEM | AAA | 24 | 303 | 42 | 20 | 1 | 2 | 31 | 37 | 49 | 12 | 2 | .275/.366/.381 |
| 2020 | STL | MLB | 25 | 17 | 1 | 0 | 0 | 1 | 1 | 0 | 6 | 0 | 0 | .176/.176/.353 |
| 2021 FS | CIN | MLB | 26 | 600 | 65 | 29 | 1 | 12 | 66 | 40 | 102 | 3 | 2 | .258/.316/.385 |
| 2021 DC | CIN | MLB | 26 | 61 | 6 | 2 | 0 | 1 | 6 | 4 | 10 | 0 | 0 | .258/.316/.385 |

Comparables: Yangervis Solarte, Nate Spears, Adrian Cardenas

Schrock has minimal power but he makes contact and gets on base, which is fine since he's a smooth lefty second baseman. The Cubs claimed him off waivers from the Cardinals early in the offseason.

| YEAR | TEAM | LVL | AGE | PA | DRC+ | BABIP | BRR | FRAA | WARP |
|------|------|-----|-----|-----|------|-------|-----|------|------|
| 2018 | MEM | AAA | 23 | 457 | 72 | .260 | -1.7 | 2B(80): -3.3, 3B(14): -0.2, LF(4): 0.5 | -1.1 |
| 2019 | MEM | AAA | 24 | 303 | 102 | .332 | -1.6 | 3B(56): -4.8, 2B(10): 0.0, LF(7): -0.1 | 0.6 |
| 2020 | STL | MLB | 25 | 17 | 81 | .200 | -0.3 | 2B(5): 0.2, 3B(2): -0.1, P(1): -0.0 | 0.0 |
| 2021 FS | CIN | MLB | 26 | 600 | 90 | .299 | -0.7 | 2B -1, 1B 0 | 0.6 |
| 2021 DC | CIN | MLB | 26 | 61 | 90 | .299 | -0.1 | 2B 0 | 0.1 |

## Michael Siani  CF

Born: 07/16/99  Age: 21  Bats: L  Throws: L
Height: 6'1"  Weight: 188  Origin: Round 4, 2018 Draft (#109 overall)

| YEAR | TEAM | LVL | AGE | PA | R | 2B | 3B | HR | RBI | BB | K | SB | CS | AVG/OBP/SLG |
|------|------|-----|-----|-----|----|----|----|----|-----|----|----|----|----|-------------|
| 2018 | GRN | ROK | 18 | 205 | 24 | 6 | 3 | 2 | 13 | 16 | 35 | 6 | 4 | .288/.351/.386 |
| 2019 | DAY | LO-A | 19 | 531 | 75 | 10 | 6 | 6 | 39 | 46 | 108 | 45 | 15 | .253/.333/.339 |
| 2021 FS | CIN | MLB | 21 | 600 | 48 | 22 | 4 | 8 | 51 | 34 | 169 | 25 | 12 | .224/.277/.324 |

Comparables: Derek Hill, Carlos Gómez, Joe Benson

Siani is a true center fielder whose speed and cannon arm will play at the highest level, but has yet to show enough power or consistency at the plate to profile as anything more than a fourth outfielder.

# Cincinnati Reds 2021

| YEAR | TEAM | LVL | AGE | PA | DRC+ | BABIP | BRR | FRAA | WARP |
|---|---|---|---|---|---|---|---|---|---|
| 2018 | GRN | ROK | 18 | 205 | | .342 | | | |
| 2019 | DAY | LO-A | 19 | 531 | 95 | .317 | 7.4 | CF(112): 24.7, RF(5): -0.7, LF(1): 0.0 | 4.8 |
| 2021 FS | CIN | MLB | 21 | 600 | 64 | .307 | 2.9 | CF 17, RF 0 | 1.1 |

## Dwight Smith   LF
Born: 10/26/92   Age: 28   Bats: L   Throws: R
Height: 6'0"   Weight: 210   Origin: Round 1, 2011 Draft (#53 overall)

| YEAR | TEAM | LVL | AGE | PA | R | 2B | 3B | HR | RBI | BB | K | SB | CS | AVG/OBP/SLG |
|---|---|---|---|---|---|---|---|---|---|---|---|---|---|---|
| 2018 | BUF | AAA | 25 | 361 | 39 | 25 | 1 | 6 | 42 | 44 | 53 | 9 | 3 | .268/.358/.413 |
| 2018 | TOR | MLB | 25 | 75 | 9 | 8 | 0 | 2 | 8 | 7 | 13 | 0 | 0 | .262/.347/.477 |
| 2019 | NOR | AAA | 26 | 49 | 9 | 2 | 0 | 3 | 12 | 3 | 8 | 0 | 0 | .311/.367/.556 |
| 2019 | BAL | MLB | 26 | 392 | 46 | 16 | 3 | 13 | 53 | 26 | 82 | 5 | 1 | .241/.297/.412 |
| 2020 | BAL | MLB | 27 | 72 | 9 | 3 | 0 | 2 | 6 | 7 | 19 | 1 | 0 | .222/.306/.365 |
| 2021 FS | CIN | MLB | 28 | 600 | 63 | 27 | 2 | 18 | 69 | 53 | 142 | 3 | 2 | .237/.312/.398 |

Comparables: Todd Hollandsworth, Chad Allen, Eric Valent

Smith has added muscle and mass over the last few years, causing him to lose speed (his 25.6 ft/sec sprint speed places him behind a few catchers) and get worse on defense, and it didn't help him add any power to the profile. Other than that, Mrs. Lincoln, how was the play?

| YEAR | TEAM | LVL | AGE | PA | DRC+ | BABIP | BRR | FRAA | WARP |
|---|---|---|---|---|---|---|---|---|---|
| 2018 | BUF | AAA | 25 | 361 | 127 | .302 | -0.3 | LF(62): 1.2, RF(14): -0.1 | 1.5 |
| 2018 | TOR | MLB | 25 | 75 | 99 | .294 | -0.4 | LF(19): -1.5, RF(6): 0.7 | 0.1 |
| 2019 | NOR | AAA | 26 | 49 | 117 | .324 | -0.1 | LF(5): -0.3, RF(2): 0.1 | 0.2 |
| 2019 | BAL | MLB | 26 | 392 | 81 | .274 | -0.1 | LF(86): -0.7 | 0.0 |
| 2020 | BAL | MLB | 27 | 72 | 85 | .279 | 0.0 | LF(16): 0.4 | -0.1 |
| 2021 FS | CIN | MLB | 28 | 600 | 93 | .289 | -0.5 | LF 1, RF 0 | 1.1 |

## Tyler Stephenson   C
Born: 08/16/96   Age: 24   Bats: R   Throws: R
Height: 6'4"   Weight: 225   Origin: Round 1, 2015 Draft (#11 overall)

| YEAR | TEAM | LVL | AGE | PA | R | 2B | 3B | HR | RBI | BB | K | SB | CS | AVG/OBP/SLG |
|---|---|---|---|---|---|---|---|---|---|---|---|---|---|---|
| 2018 | DAY | HI-A | 21 | 450 | 60 | 20 | 1 | 11 | 59 | 45 | 98 | 1 | 0 | .250/.338/.392 |
| 2019 | CHA | AA | 22 | 363 | 47 | 19 | 1 | 6 | 44 | 37 | 60 | 0 | 0 | .285/.372/.410 |
| 2020 | CIN | MLB | 23 | 20 | 4 | 0 | 0 | 2 | 6 | 2 | 9 | 0 | 0 | .294/.400/.647 |
| 2021 FS | CIN | MLB | 24 | 600 | 65 | 24 | 1 | 18 | 67 | 49 | 184 | 0 | 1 | .222/.297/.376 |
| 2021 DC | CIN | MLB | 24 | 256 | 28 | 10 | 0 | 7 | 28 | 21 | 78 | 0 | 0 | .222/.297/.376 |

Comparables: Jason Castro, Alex Avila, Christian Vázquez

A former first-rounder out of a Georgia high school back in what feels like the cretaceous period, Stephenson has overcome more misfortune than a Coen Brothers protagonist to finally make a splash in Cincinnati. His debut couldn't have gone much better, as Stephenson went deep in his first at bat and showed great promise down the stretch. Tall for a catcher, Stephenson nevertheless blocks and receives well enough to succeed and if he can improve his throwing he could become an above-average defender. At the plate he has both patience and power but his hit tool is nothing to write home about, all of which adds up to a potential plus bat behind the dish. Although he's entering his age-24 season, Stephenson has put in only one half-season in the high minors and would benefit from some time in Triple-A. If he can stay healthy he has the skills to be a frontline big-league catcher.

| YEAR | TEAM | P. COUNT | FRM RUNS | BLK RUNS | THRW RUNS | TOT RUNS |
|---|---|---|---|---|---|---|
| 2020 | CIN | 396 | 0.0 | 0.0 | 0.0 | 0.0 |
| 2021 | CIN | 7215 | 0.6 | 0.5 | 0.2 | 1.3 |
| 2021 | CIN | 7215 | 0.6 | 0.5 | 0.2 | 1.3 |

| YEAR | TEAM | LVL | AGE | PA | DRC+ | BABIP | BRR | FRAA | WARP |
|---|---|---|---|---|---|---|---|---|---|
| 2018 | DAY | HI-A | 21 | 450 | 116 | .301 | 0.2 | C(97): -3.3 | 1.5 |
| 2019 | CHA | AA | 22 | 363 | 128 | .331 | -2.1 | C(87): -11.8 | 1.3 |
| 2020 | CIN | MLB | 23 | 20 | 80 | .500 | 0.0 | C(4): -0.0 | 0.0 |
| 2021 FS | CIN | MLB | 24 | 600 | 83 | .301 | -0.9 | C 2 | 1.3 |
| 2021 DC | CIN | MLB | 24 | 256 | 83 | .301 | -0.4 | C 1, 1B 0 | 0.4 |

# Cincinnati Reds 2021

## Dee Strange-Gordon  2B
Born: 04/22/88   Age: 33   Bats: L   Throws: R
Height: 5'11"   Weight: 166   Origin: Round 4, 2008 Draft (#127 overall)

| YEAR | TEAM | LVL | AGE | PA | R | 2B | 3B | HR | RBI | BB | K | SB | CS | AVG/OBP/SLG |
|---|---|---|---|---|---|---|---|---|---|---|---|---|---|---|
| 2018 | SEA | MLB | 30 | 588 | 62 | 17 | 8 | 4 | 36 | 9 | 80 | 30 | 12 | .268/.288/.349 |
| 2019 | SEA | MLB | 31 | 421 | 36 | 12 | 6 | 3 | 34 | 18 | 61 | 22 | 5 | .275/.304/.359 |
| 2020 | SEA | MLB | 32 | 82 | 12 | 1 | 0 | 0 | 3 | 5 | 13 | 3 | 2 | .200/.268/.213 |
| 2021 FS | CIN | MLB | 33 | 600 | 50 | 21 | 4 | 7 | 53 | 25 | 104 | 36 | 12 | *.260/.298/.353* |

Comparables: Tony Womack, Julian Javier, Joe Inglett

    For many, the love of baseball is rooted in the analysis of numbers. For them, Dee Strange-Gordon's time in Seattle is an easy bust. He was brought to Seattle as an experiment: Could a highly athletic, established major league middle-infielder be converted into an outfielder on the fly? Due to Robinson Canó's suspension in 2018, we never really found out, although early returns pointed to "probably not." Strange-Gordon arrived in Seattle along with international slot money the Mariners had ear-marked for their failed pursuit of Shohei Othani. He arrived to help the team end the longest playoff absence in major American sports find the postseason. They did not. So many failures—small and large, personal and organizational—ripple from Strange-Gordon's time in the Emerald City.

    So it's up to you if that's how you would like to think of him. That's how we normally do it as baseball fans. The name on the back of the jersey failed the name on the front, and in so doing hollowed out the man in between the two. Before we participate in that same old exercise here, however, we should acknowledge that amidst all that failure Strange-Gordon was a far, far, better teammate and humanitarian than he was a baseball player in Seattle. His advocacy for local charities, his willingness to mentor, advise, and assist younger teammates (even those brought in to replace him), and his willingness to speak out on domestic violence, mental health, and other issues haunting American life stand, at minimum, alongside what he did between the foul lines.

    That Strange-Gordon spent his time in Seattle struggling to do his job well is the reality we usually talk about here. Often we'd use it as a cudgel to grind some axe against an executive, cite something about inefficiencies, and maybe make a bad pun. We'll still do that plenty, but that the quality of the player never once affected the quality of the man is something worthy of praise, and well overdue praise at that.

| YEAR | TEAM | LVL | AGE | PA | DRC+ | BABIP | BRR | FRAA | WARP |
|---|---|---|---|---|---|---|---|---|---|
| 2018 | SEA | MLB | 30 | 588 | 75 | .304 | 4.2 | 2B(81): 2.5, CF(53): 0.7, SS(8): -0.4 | 0.9 |
| 2019 | SEA | MLB | 31 | 421 | 78 | .313 | 2.2 | 2B(111): 0.5, SS(2): 0.2 | 0.5 |
| 2020 | SEA | MLB | 32 | 82 | 75 | .242 | 0.1 | 2B(13): -1.7, LF(13): 0.7, SS(3): -0.4 | -0.2 |
| 2021 FS | CIN | MLB | 33 | 600 | 76 | .307 | 3.6 | 2B 0, CF 2 | 0.6 |

## Brandon Bailey  RHP

Born: 10/19/94   Age: 26   Bats: R   Throws: R
Height: 5'10"   Weight: 195   Origin: Round 6, 2016 Draft (#172 overall)

| YEAR | TEAM | LVL | AGE | W | L | SV | G | GS | IP | H | HR | BB/9 | K/9 | K | GB% | BABIP |
|---|---|---|---|---|---|---|---|---|---|---|---|---|---|---|---|---|
| 2018 | FAY | HI-A | 23 | 5 | 8 | 0 | 20 | 16 | $97^2$ | 69 | 6 | 4.0 | 10.4 | 113 | 37.9% | .270 |
| 2018 | CC | AA | 23 | 1 | 0 | 1 | 5 | 1 | $24^2$ | 21 | 5 | 3.3 | 8.4 | 23 | 37.5% | .239 |
| 2019 | CC | AA | 24 | 4 | 5 | 0 | 22 | 17 | $92^2$ | 72 | 12 | 4.0 | 10.0 | 103 | 36.4% | .268 |
| 2020 | HOU | MLB | 25 | 0 | 0 | 0 | 5 | 0 | $7^1$ | 6 | 1 | 3.7 | 4.9 | 4 | 31.8% | .238 |
| 2021 FS | CIN | MLB | 26 | 2 | 3 | 0 | 57 | 0 | 50 | 48 | 9 | 4.5 | 9.1 | 50 | 35.5% | .292 |
| 2021 DC | CIN | MLB | 26 | 3 | 3 | 0 | 32 | 4 | 37.7 | 36 | 7 | 4.5 | 9.1 | 38 | 35.5% | .292 |

Comparables: Tyler Wilson, Dane Dunning, Jonathan Holder

Nobody will be shocked to learn that Bailey's low-90s fastball plays up because of a high spin rate—an apparent prerequisite for Houston pitching prospects. What sets Bailey apart from most of the other bullpen debutants is the depth of his arsenal. He threw five distinct offerings in his brief glimpse of the majors, a relic from spending the majority of his pro career as a starter. He lacks the durability and efficiency to do so at the highest level, but he should go on bailing out other starters in multi-inning outings with his diverse range of looks.

| YEAR | TEAM | LVL | AGE | WHIP | ERA | DRA- | WARP | MPH | FB% | WHF | CSP |
|---|---|---|---|---|---|---|---|---|---|---|---|
| 2018 | FAY | HI-A | 23 | 1.15 | 2.49 | 52 | 3.2 | | | | |
| 2018 | CC | AA | 23 | 1.22 | 4.01 | 50 | 0.7 | | | | |
| 2019 | CC | AA | 24 | 1.22 | 3.30 | 86 | 0.8 | | | | |
| 2020 | HOU | MLB | 25 | 1.23 | 2.45 | 127 | 0.0 | 93.5 | 61.9% | 23.4% | |
| 2021 FS | CIN | MLB | 26 | 1.47 | 5.10 | 110 | 0.0 | 93.5 | 61.9% | 23.4% | 48.2% |
| 2021 DC | CIN | MLB | 26 | 1.47 | 5.10 | 110 | 0.0 | 93.5 | 61.9% | 23.4% | 48.2% |

# Cincinnati Reds 2021

## Jesse Biddle  LHP
Born: 10/22/91  Age: 29  Bats: L  Throws: L
Height: 6'5"  Weight: 220  Origin: Round 1, 2010 Draft (#27 overall)

| YEAR | TEAM | LVL | AGE | W | L | SV | G | GS | IP | H | HR | BB/9 | K/9 | K | GB% | BABIP |
|---|---|---|---|---|---|---|---|---|---|---|---|---|---|---|---|---|
| 2018 | GWN | AAA | 26 | 0 | 0 | 1 | 4 | 0 | $6^1$ | 3 | 0 | 1.4 | 11.4 | 8 | 23.1% | .231 |
| 2018 | ATL | MLB | 26 | 6 | 1 | 1 | 60 | 0 | $63^2$ | 50 | 6 | 4.4 | 9.5 | 67 | 55.2% | .280 |
| 2019 | GWN | AAA | 27 | 1 | 0 | 0 | 4 | 0 | $5^1$ | 6 | 1 | 1.7 | 10.1 | 6 | 40.0% | .385 |
| 2019 | ATL | MLB | 27 | 0 | 1 | 0 | 15 | 0 | $11^2$ | 18 | 1 | 7.7 | 8.5 | 11 | 39.5% | .405 |
| 2019 | SEA | MLB | 27 | 0 | 0 | 0 | 11 | 0 | 11 | 20 | 2 | 5.7 | 6.5 | 8 | 40.9% | .429 |
| 2019 | TEX | MLB | 27 | 0 | 0 | 0 | 4 | 0 | $5^1$ | 4 | 2 | 8.4 | 11.8 | 7 | 69.2% | .182 |
| 2020 | CIN | MLB | 28 | 0 | 0 | 0 | 1 | 0 | $0^2$ | 1 | 0 | 13.5 | 13.5 | 1 | 100.0% | .500 |
| 2021 FS | CIN | MLB | 29 | 2 | 3 | 0 | 57 | 0 | 50 | 48 | 7 | 5.1 | 8.9 | 49 | 47.4% | .300 |

Comparables: Jason Adam, Austin Brice, Caleb Smith

Biddle only made one appearance for the Reds before shoulder woes once again shelved him, the latest in a series of unfortunate events—including a hailstorm-induced concussion—that have derailed the former top prospect during a career most notable for its dogged perseverance. Having turned down a minor-league assignment, he'll have to persevere elsewhere.

| YEAR | TEAM | LVL | AGE | WHIP | ERA | DRA- | WARP | MPH | FB% | WHF | CSP |
|---|---|---|---|---|---|---|---|---|---|---|---|
| 2018 | GWN | AAA | 26 | 0.63 | 0.00 | 48 | 0.2 | | | | |
| 2018 | ATL | MLB | 26 | 1.27 | 3.11 | 91 | 0.6 | 96.2 | 55.2% | 25.9% | |
| 2019 | GWN | AAA | 27 | 1.31 | 3.38 | 74 | 0.1 | | | | |
| 2019 | ATL | MLB | 27 | 2.40 | 5.40 | 109 | 0.0 | 95.4 | 52.5% | 23.5% | |
| 2019 | SEA | MLB | 27 | 2.45 | 9.82 | 173 | -0.4 | 95.3 | 64.6% | 17.0% | |
| 2019 | TEX | MLB | 27 | 1.69 | 11.81 | 164 | -0.2 | 94.4 | 41.7% | 27.9% | |
| 2020 | CIN | MLB | 28 | 3.00 | 0.00 | 80 | 0.0 | 97.2 | 45.0% | 11.1% | |
| 2021 FS | CIN | MLB | 29 | 1.53 | 4.93 | 108 | 0.0 | 95.7 | 54.8% | 23.4% | 49.0% |

## Edgar García  RHP

Born: 10/04/96  Age: 24  Bats: R  Throws: R
Height: 6'1"  Weight: 205  Origin: International Free Agent, 2014

| YEAR | TEAM | LVL | AGE | W | L | SV | G | GS | IP | H | HR | BB/9 | K/9 | K | GB% | BABIP |
|---|---|---|---|---|---|---|---|---|---|---|---|---|---|---|---|---|
| 2018 | REA | AA | 21 | 7 | 2 | 8 | 47 | 0 | 59$^2$ | 45 | 6 | 3.8 | 10.3 | 68 | 38.7% | .264 |
| 2019 | LHV | AAA | 22 | 2 | 1 | 8 | 25 | 0 | 29 | 15 | 4 | 2.5 | 11.8 | 38 | 29.5% | .193 |
| 2019 | PHI | MLB | 22 | 2 | 0 | 0 | 37 | 0 | 39 | 38 | 11 | 6.0 | 10.2 | 44 | 32.7% | .300 |
| 2020 | TB | MLB | 23 | 0 | 0 | 1 | 4 | 0 | 3$^1$ | 3 | 2 | 10.8 | 2.7 | 1 | 27.3% | .111 |
| 2021 FS | CIN | MLB | 24 | 2 | 3 | 0 | 57 | 0 | 50 | 47 | 9 | 5.3 | 9.6 | 53 | 34.8% | .290 |
| 2021 DC | CIN | MLB | 24 | 1 | 1 | 0 | 29 | 0 | 24.3 | 23 | 4 | 5.3 | 9.6 | 26 | 34.8% | .290 |

Comparables: Joe Jiménez, Carter Capps, Chris Perez

Garcia is a young, hard-hurling reliever who has multiple option years remaining. It was perplexing, then, that the Phillies decided he was an expandable piece of their 40-player roster without so much as giving him an audition in the traveling house-of-horrors that was their 2020 bullpen. We'd joke that Garcia paid homage to his old teammates by giving up four runs in three innings with the Rays, but by the time you read this he'll probably have bumped his command grade enough to become a legitimate big-league reliever.

| YEAR | TEAM | LVL | AGE | WHIP | ERA | DRA- | WARP | MPH | FB% | WHF | CSP |
|---|---|---|---|---|---|---|---|---|---|---|---|
| 2018 | REA | AA | 21 | 1.17 | 3.32 | 56 | 1.6 | | | | |
| 2019 | LHV | AAA | 22 | 0.79 | 2.48 | 41 | 1.2 | | | | |
| 2019 | PHI | MLB | 22 | 1.64 | 5.77 | 119 | -0.2 | 95.5 | 49.7% | 32.1% | |
| 2020 | TB | MLB | 23 | 2.10 | 10.80 | 148 | -0.1 | 94.0 | 52.4% | 16.7% | |
| 2021 FS | CIN | MLB | 24 | 1.53 | 5.26 | 111 | -0.1 | 95.3 | 50.0% | 30.3% | 38.9% |
| 2021 DC | CIN | MLB | 24 | 1.53 | 5.26 | 111 | 0.0 | 95.3 | 50.0% | 30.3% | 38.9% |

# Cincinnati Reds 2021

## Hunter Greene  RHP
Born: 08/06/99   Age: 21   Bats: R   Throws: R
Height: 6'4"   Weight: 215   Origin: Round 1, 2017 Draft (#2 overall)

| YEAR | TEAM | LVL | AGE | W | L | SV | G | GS | IP | H | HR | BB/9 | K/9 | K | GB% | BABIP |
|---|---|---|---|---|---|---|---|---|---|---|---|---|---|---|---|---|
| 2018 | DAY | LO-A | 18 | 3 | 7 | 0 | 18 | 18 | 68$^1$ | 66 | 6 | 3.0 | 11.7 | 89 | 42.6% | .355 |
| 2021 | | | | | | | | | No projection | | | | | | | |

Comparables: Kolby Allard, Roberto Osuna, Jordan Lyles

When Baseball Prospectus co-founder Gary Huckabay coined the term TINSTAAPP (There Is No Such Thing As A Pitching Prospect), he specifically had talented but untested high school pitchers like Greene in mind. Of course Greene absolutely exists, and absolutely is a pitching prospect, but the concern Huckabay was expressing about the high risks associated with drafting prep arms still apply. Since the Reds tabbed him with the second pick of the 2017 draft and decided his future lay on the mound rather than at shortstop, Greene has only thrown 73 professional innings before the combination of Tommy John surgery and Donny John plague sidelined him for more than two full seasons. The fireballing Californian should be lighting up radar guns again this summer, but there's still the matter of sorting out his secondaries, gaining command, mastering the art of pitch sequencing, conquering the upper minors and maintaining arm health before we'll know whether Greene's estimable stuff can ever shine in a big-league rotation.

| YEAR | TEAM | LVL | AGE | WHIP | ERA | DRA- | WARP | MPH | FB% | WHF | CSP |
|---|---|---|---|---|---|---|---|---|---|---|---|
| 2018 | DAY | LO-A | 18 | 1.30 | 4.48 | 79 | 1.2 | | | | |
| 2021 | | | | | | No projection | | | | | |

## Ryan Hendrix  RHP
Born: 12/16/94   Age: 26   Bats: R   Throws: R
Height: 6'3"   Weight: 215   Origin: Round 5, 2016 Draft (#138 overall)

| YEAR | TEAM | LVL | AGE | W | L | SV | G | GS | IP | H | HR | BB/9 | K/9 | K | GB% | BABIP |
|---|---|---|---|---|---|---|---|---|---|---|---|---|---|---|---|---|
| 2018 | DAY | HI-A | 23 | 4 | 4 | 12 | 44 | 0 | 51 | 38 | 2 | 4.6 | 13.9 | 79 | 49.5% | .340 |
| 2019 | RED | ROK | 24 | 1 | 0 | 0 | 4 | 2 | 5 | 1 | 0 | 0.0 | 14.4 | 8 | 44.4% | .111 |
| 2019 | CHA | AA | 24 | 3 | 0 | 2 | 16 | 0 | 19$^1$ | 14 | 0 | 3.7 | 10.7 | 23 | 43.8% | .292 |
| 2021 FS | CIN | MLB | 26 | 2 | 2 | 0 | 57 | 0 | 50 | 42 | 7 | 5.0 | 10.4 | 58 | 41.6% | .284 |
| 2021 DC | CIN | MLB | 26 | 1 | 1 | 0 | 35 | 0 | 18.3 | 15 | 2 | 5.0 | 10.4 | 21 | 41.6% | .284 |

Comparables: David Bednar, Stephen Nogosek, JD Hammer

Aggie alumnus Hendrix deploys mid-90s heat and a power curve in aid of the killer strikeout rates that portend success in a big league bullpen and the medium-bad walk rates that point to the middle innings.

| YEAR | TEAM | LVL | AGE | WHIP | ERA | DRA- | WARP | MPH | FB% | WHF | CSP |
|---|---|---|---|---|---|---|---|---|---|---|---|
| 2018 | DAY | HI-A | 23 | 1.25 | 1.76 | 56 | 1.3 | | | | |
| 2019 | RED | ROK | 24 | 0.20 | 0.00 | | | | | | |
| 2019 | CHA | AA | 24 | 1.14 | 2.33 | 82 | 0.1 | | | | |
| 2021 FS | CIN | MLB | 26 | 1.41 | 4.37 | 98 | 0.3 | | | | |
| 2021 DC | CIN | MLB | 26 | 1.41 | 4.37 | 98 | 0.1 | | | | |

## Joel Kuhnel   RHP

Born: 02/19/95   Age: 26   Bats: R   Throws: R
Height: 6'4"   Weight: 280   Origin: Round 11, 2016 Draft (#318 overall)

| YEAR | TEAM | LVL | AGE | W | L | SV | G | GS | IP | H | HR | BB/9 | K/9 | K | GB% | BABIP |
|---|---|---|---|---|---|---|---|---|---|---|---|---|---|---|---|---|
| 2018 | DAY | HI-A | 23 | 1 | 4 | 17 | 44 | 0 | 53$^1$ | 54 | 2 | 1.9 | 9.4 | 56 | 51.0% | .347 |
| 2019 | CHA | AA | 24 | 3 | 2 | 10 | 25 | 0 | 35$^2$ | 26 | 5 | 2.0 | 7.6 | 30 | 39.4% | .212 |
| 2019 | LOU | AAA | 24 | 2 | 1 | 4 | 16 | 0 | 18 | 13 | 1 | 4.0 | 10.0 | 20 | 37.8% | .273 |
| 2019 | CIN | MLB | 24 | 1 | 0 | 0 | 11 | 0 | 9$^2$ | 8 | 1 | 4.7 | 8.4 | 9 | 53.6% | .259 |
| 2020 | CIN | MLB | 25 | 1 | 0 | 0 | 3 | 0 | 3 | 4 | 2 | 0.0 | 9.0 | 3 | 30.0% | .250 |
| 2021 FS | CIN | MLB | 26 | 2 | 2 | 0 | 57 | 0 | 50 | 49 | 8 | 3.0 | 8.0 | 44 | 39.1% | .288 |

Comparables: Sam Tuivailala, Jensen Lewis, Bruce Rondón

Kuhnel is a Texas-sized Longhorn alum who strives to bait 'em with his mid-90s heat and hook 'em with his plus slider, but he'll need to improve his fastball command if he wants to target the big fish.

| YEAR | TEAM | LVL | AGE | WHIP | ERA | DRA- | WARP | MPH | FB% | WHF | CSP |
|---|---|---|---|---|---|---|---|---|---|---|---|
| 2018 | DAY | HI-A | 23 | 1.22 | 3.04 | 73 | 0.8 | | | | |
| 2019 | CHA | AA | 24 | 0.95 | 2.27 | 66 | 0.6 | | | | |
| 2019 | LOU | AAA | 24 | 1.17 | 2.00 | 70 | 0.5 | | | | |
| 2019 | CIN | MLB | 24 | 1.34 | 4.66 | 89 | 0.1 | 98.3 | 61.4% | 29.4% | |
| 2020 | CIN | MLB | 25 | 1.33 | 6.00 | 102 | 0.0 | 98.0 | 57.9% | 15.8% | |
| 2021 FS | CIN | MLB | 26 | 1.32 | 4.29 | 97 | 0.3 | 98.2 | 60.2% | 24.8% | 44.4% |

# Cincinnati Reds 2021

## Nick Lodolo  LHP
Born: 02/05/98  Age: 23  Bats: L  Throws: L
Height: 6'6"  Weight: 205  Origin: Round 1, 2019 Draft (#7 overall)

| YEAR | TEAM | LVL | AGE | W | L | SV | G | GS | IP | H | HR | BB/9 | K/9 | K | GB% | BABIP |
|---|---|---|---|---|---|---|---|---|---|---|---|---|---|---|---|---|
| 2019 | BIL | ROK+ | 21 | 0 | 1 | 0 | 6 | 6 | 11$^1$ | 12 | 1 | 0.0 | 16.7 | 21 | 32.0% | .458 |
| 2019 | DAY | LO-A | 21 | 0 | 0 | 0 | 2 | 2 | 7 | 6 | 0 | 0.0 | 11.6 | 9 | 50.0% | .333 |
| 2021 FS | CIN | MLB | 23 | 2 | 3 | 0 | 57 | 0 | 50 | 48 | 7 | 4.2 | 7.8 | 43 | 38.2% | .286 |

Comparables: Patrick Sandoval, Cristian Javier, Kris Bubic

   The lack of a minor league season was clearly an impediment to the development of young pitchers like Lodolo. On the bright side, it also means that Lodolo's 2019 debut numbers remain his only numbers, so his impeccable 30:0 career professional strikeout-to-walk ratio remains intact. Drafted out of TCU with the seventh-overall pick in 2019, Lodolo is a tall lefty with mid-90s heat, a sharp slider, a plus change and a proven ability to throw strikes. His combination of stuff and polish give him a high floor, and after spending a year with pitching coordinator Kyle Boddy and his Driveline techniques who knows what his ceiling might become.

| YEAR | TEAM | LVL | AGE | WHIP | ERA | DRA- | WARP | MPH | FB% | WHF | CSP |
|---|---|---|---|---|---|---|---|---|---|---|---|
| 2019 | BIL | ROK+ | 21 | 1.06 | 2.38 | | | | | | |
| 2019 | DAY | LO-A | 21 | 0.86 | 2.57 | 69 | 0.1 | | | | |
| 2021 FS | CIN | MLB | 23 | 1.44 | 4.84 | 112 | -0.1 | | | | |

## Tony Santillan  RHP
Born: 04/15/97  Age: 24  Bats: R  Throws: R
Height: 6'3"  Weight: 240  Origin: Round 2, 2015 Draft (#49 overall)

| YEAR | TEAM | LVL | AGE | W | L | SV | G | GS | IP | H | HR | BB/9 | K/9 | K | GB% | BABIP |
|---|---|---|---|---|---|---|---|---|---|---|---|---|---|---|---|---|
| 2018 | DAY | HI-A | 21 | 6 | 4 | 0 | 15 | 15 | 86$^2$ | 81 | 5 | 2.3 | 7.6 | 73 | 42.3% | .302 |
| 2018 | PNS | AA | 21 | 4 | 3 | 0 | 11 | 11 | 62$^1$ | 65 | 8 | 2.3 | 8.8 | 61 | 43.9% | .318 |
| 2019 | CHA | AA | 22 | 2 | 8 | 0 | 21 | 21 | 102$^1$ | 110 | 8 | 4.7 | 8.1 | 92 | 32.8% | .342 |
| 2021 FS | CIN | MLB | 24 | 2 | 3 | 0 | 57 | 0 | 50 | 48 | 9 | 5.1 | 7.7 | 42 | 37.3% | .281 |
| 2021 DC | CIN | MLB | 24 | 5 | 4 | 0 | 40 | 6 | 56.7 | 55 | 10 | 5.1 | 7.7 | 48 | 37.3% | .281 |

Comparables: Touki Toussaint, Miguel Almonte, Jonathan Hernández

   Let's hope the industrial-sized Santillan gets another opportunity to finally post a solid season in a Double-A rotation this summer; his fastball/slider combo can flash plus, but his iffy changeup will determine whether he's destined for the bullpen.

| YEAR | TEAM | LVL | AGE | WHIP | ERA | DRA- | WARP | MPH | FB% | WHF | CSP |
|---|---|---|---|---|---|---|---|---|---|---|---|
| 2018 | DAY | HI-A | 21 | 1.19 | 2.70 | 105 | 0.2 | | | | |
| 2018 | PNS | AA | 21 | 1.30 | 3.61 | 88 | 0.8 | | | | |
| 2019 | CHA | AA | 22 | 1.60 | 4.84 | 118 | -1.0 | | | | |
| *2021 FS* | *CIN* | *MLB* | *24* | *1.55* | *5.31* | *117* | *-0.2* | | | | |
| *2021 DC* | *CIN* | *MLB* | *24* | *1.55* | *5.31* | *117* | *-0.1* | | | | |

# Reds Prospects

## The State of the System:
The Reds' system feels like a bit of a hodgepodge of player types, a mishmash of developmental preferences, but it's a fairly deep system at least.

## The Top Ten:

**1** ── ★ ★ ★ *2021 Top 101 Prospect* **#57** ★ ★ ★ ──
**Nick Lodolo   LHP**     OFP: 60    ETA: 2022, maybe late 2021 if necessary
Born: 02/05/98   Age: 23   Bats: L   Throws: L   Height: 6'6"   Weight: 205
Origin: Round 1, 2019 Draft (#7 overall)

**The Report:** A well-regarded SoCal prep arm out of high school, Lodolo spurned the Pirates in 2016 as the 41st-overall pick and instead attended TCU. The tall, lanky lefty had mixed success his first two years, finally filling out and taking off in his junior season. With a fastball that sits comfortably in the low-to-mid 90s, his repeatable delivery allows for very good command of all his pitches, making each of the individual pitch grades play up. His breaking ball can be manipulated to be a short slider or more slurvy with downer action, while the changeup has good fade and is sold with deceptive arm speed. A workhorse body, clean mechanics, at least three distinct pitches with command of each all equate to a high-end starter worthy of the top 10 selection a year ago.

**Development Track:** There should be some reluctance to mess too much with a guy who has above-average stuff and can throw quality strikes. If there is one knock against Lodolo, he's never been a "Statcast star" with high spin rates. What he does offer is a wide release point that creates a tough angle to the plate. So while there might be more to unlock with his spin efficiency or tinkering with grips, making sure it's not a significant detriment to what he already does well will be advantageous.

**Variance:** Medium. There is a fair amount of polish with perhaps a slightly limited ceiling, but you trade that off for an elevated floor.

**J.P. Breen's Fantasy Take:** Lodolo gets more love in some dynasty circles than his scouting report might warrant, due to his 30-to-zero strikeout-to-walk rate as a professional. He's more of a potential mid-rotation workhorse than a top-end fantasy star, as currently constructed, but that could change with arsenal tweaks or increased spin rates. I love the frame and the high floor, but he's a fringe top-101 dynasty prospect and is on the outside of my personal Top 101.

# Cincinnati Reds 2021

**2** **Austin Hendrick**  CF   OFP: 60   ETA: 2023
Born: 06/15/01  Age: 20  Bats: L  Throws: L  Height: 6'0"  Weight: 195
Origin: Round 1, 2020 Draft (#12 overall)

**The Report:** During the big national high school showcases last summer, Hendrick did everything possible to vault himself into the first round as one of the top hitters in the class. Displaying huge raw power from the left side despite standing a listed 6-foot tall, Hendrick is able to generate a ton of bat speed due to his explosive hands. He tends to over-swing, however, causing his mechanics to break down. Pitch recognition might be the issue, as he stays within himself when he's on time. A solid outfielder with enough arm, he profiles best as a future right fielder, but will likely be given a chance to start his pro career in center.

**Development Track:** Scouts began noticing subtle tweaks to his swing between the high profile all-star events and his travel-ball squad in the fall. Depending on when he was seen, his hand load or stride or foot alignment would be different. Some believed it was a knock against him, others pointed to the fact he was open to coaching and capable of working through new ideas. Either way, his present ability to get natural lift on the ball fits perfectly into the Reds' hitting philosophy, and only needs to find the mechanical tweak that works consistently for him.

**Variance:** Extreme. Your typical boom-or-bust type who will either slug in the middle of the order or swing-and-miss too much to reach full potential.

**J.P. Breen's Fantasy Take:** As Gwen Stefani would say, this my s--t, this my s--t. Hendrick possesses some of the best raw power in the minors, but it comes with typical concerns about contact rates and pitch recognition. While I typically advocate shying away from these popular boom-or-bust power hitters, as homers are no longer difficult to obtain on the cheap, I'm a sucker for potential superstars who come from geographic areas that are not baseball powerhouses. When they blossom, it happens in the blink of an eye. Hendrick is one of the few guys outside the top-75 dynasty prospects who has a clear path to becoming a top-25 dynasty prospect with a good few months in 2021.

**3** **Hunter Greene**  RHP   OFP: 55   ETA: 2023
Born: 08/06/99  Age: 21  Bats: R  Throws: R  Height: 6'4"  Weight: 215
Origin: Round 1, 2017 Draft (#2 overall)

**The Report:** Greene was a two-way prospect out of southern California with 1.1 buzz going into the 2017 draft. He ended up going second overall—although received the biggest bonus—and the Reds quickly had him ditch the shortstop's glove to become a full-time moundsman. It wasn't hard to see why. Greene regularly hit triple digits from an athletic, repeatable delivery. He also showed some feel for a slider. Not much has changed since draft day though. Well, one major thing has: He has a new elbow scar from his 2019 Tommy John surgery. The elite arm speed remains, but the fastball runs rather true, and the slider that flashes plus often required him to slow down his arm to really snap it off.

**Development Track:** Greene was throwing at the alternate site—and getting the fastball back into the high-90s. For a high pick from 2017, he's a ways behind the development curve now due to injury and 2020 being a year where it would be awfully bold of you to fly the Goodyear blimp. None of that really matters if his velocity comes all the way back and the secondaries continue to improve—he's added a cutter, and taken quickly to it—but many of the same questions about the profile remain two years later. The good news is he is healthy and throwing without restrictions.

**Variance:** High. Given the injury and missed development time, Greene could still go in a number of directions as a prospect. While this is true of all prospects that dealt with a functionally lost season, it's especially true of Greene: We'll know a lot more after 2021.

**J.P. Breen's Fantasy Take:** The name of the dynasty game with minor-league starters is upside. Given that, I'd rather have Greene than Lodolo in standard dynasty leagues. If the velocity returns and the new cutter is as legit as it sounds, Greene has SP2 projection with room for more. While the injury risk is real and the variance in ultimate outcomes is extreme, there are few pitching prospects with the top-end upside that Greene boasts. That's all I care about.

### 4 Tyler Stephenson   C     OFP: 55   ETA: Debuted in 2020
Born: 08/16/96   Age: 24   Bats: R   Throws: R   Height: 6'4"   Weight: 225
Origin: Round 1, 2015 Draft (#11 overall)

**The Report:** We've been writing about Stephenson for more than half a decade now. The good news is we are no longer writing about his injury issues, and the healthy seasons now outnumber the IL-plagued ones. He remains on the larger side for a catcher with commensurate defensive concerns. The arm strength is average but he can be slow to get the ball out. His receiving has improved, but he'll never be super flexible or athletic behind the plate. He projects well enough defensively that you will want to get his bat into the lineup if it plays to the 50 hit, 55 power baked into his OFP below.

**Development Track:** Stephenson made his major-league debut in 2020 while Tucker Barnhart was on paternity leave. He left quite the impression in his brief appearance. It was a Third Wave Japanese Siphon Machine cup of joe, as he popped two home runs in just 20 plate appearances—including a massive bomb to center in his first major-league at-bat. He also struck out nine times, so you can't exactly say the hit tool concerns have been assuaged, but you can't really say anything about 20 plate appearances. Curt Casali is a trendy trade/non-tender candidate this offseason, so Stephenson could find himself with a relatively clean shot at a time share with Gold Glover Barnhart. He is very unlikely to be as good a defender, but he might be good enough back there to justify getting the bat in the lineup 4-5 days a week.

**Variance:** Medium. The bat looks major-league ready, but the jury will remain out on the glove until he gets a longer look in Triple-A or our new robot ump overlords arrive.

**J.P. Breen's Fantasy Take:** The scouting reports have long referenced Stephenson's raw power. However, it has rarely shown up in games. Prior to 2020, the 24-year-old had never clubbed more than 11 homers in a season, and his highest ISO (min. 100 PA) was .142. Although he showed some massive power in his brief big-league debut in 2020, it came with significant swing-and-miss issues. We're left with questions about Stephenson's hit tool and his in-game power. Thus, Stephenson is not a top-500 dynasty guy at this point, especially without a path to short-term playing time, but his proximity to the big leagues probably makes him worth a stash in leagues that roster 200-plus prospects.

**5** **Jose Garcia   SS**      OFP: 55   ETA: Debuted in 2020, might be best if you see him again in 2022
Born: 04/05/98   Age: 23   Bats: R   Throws: R   Height: 6'2"   Weight: 175
Origin: International Free Agent, 2017

**The Report:** Signed out of Cuba as a teenager, Garcia was on a fairly normal development track that featured a breakout 2019 that left him just off last year's Top 101. The bat caught up with the glove in Daytona, although he didn't (and doesn't) project for much power due to an approach that is contact-heavy over loft. The defense isn't spectacular at shortstop, but Garcia does everything well. He's rangy with good hands and has a strong arm that is accurate on the move.

**Development Track:** Perhaps the Reds called Garcia up this year because they were hoping he would give their rather anemic 2020 lineup a spark beyond what Freddy Galvis and Kyle Farmer had offered. That was a fairly large ask of a glove-over-bat prospect who hadn't seen a single plate appearance in the upper minors. And indeed, Garcia looked like he was just trying to stay above water, prioritizing contact of any sort over driving the ball, and not even making that much contact. He looked overmatched and his swing was mechanical. None of this is a death knell to an above-average projection, and I don't even know that he's a markedly different prospect than he was at this time last year. The bat just wasn't major-league ready. His glove was more or less as advertised, though.

**Variance:** High. It's unusual that we are putting high variance on a prospect who already debuted in the majors, but most prospects don't jump right from the Florida State League to the bigs. It's not a surprise Garcia was overwhelmed at the plate, but his track record of hitting in the minors isn't particularly long either. It's not a long-term worry, but he will need more consolidation time in Double- and/or Triple-A despite the Reds having an opening for a 2021 shortstop.

**J.P. Breen's Fantasy Take:** Some dynasty owners adore Garcia, arguing that he possesses more power potential than his numbers have shown to this point. For my money, I am confident in neither his power nor his approach. His walk rates perennially have been low, and his brief big-league appearance did nothing to assuage those concerns. While he's not a top-100 dynasty prospect, his glove-and-speed combo gives him a reasonable dynasty floor. He's comfortably in the Top 150.

### 6 Jonathan India  3B    OFP: 55   ETA: 2021
Born: 12/15/96   Age: 24   Bats: R   Throws: R   Height: 6'0"   Weight: 200
Origin: Round 1, 2018 Draft (#5 overall)

**The Report:** India's core skills have been steady throughout college and his time in pro ball. He's a good glove on the dirt and has a nice on-base profile in terms of his willingness to take a walk and a decent feel to hit. Unfortunately, other than his college draft year, he hasn't shown nearly the power you'd like to elevate his profile above that of a steady contributor, and it didn't show up in Double-A or the Arizona Fall League, where he should have easily outclassed his competition.

**Development Track:** His 2019 Double-A numbers are better in some ways than they look—DRC+ reminds us the Southern League is a tough place to hit, and he certainly got on base plenty. We again heard good things about his approach at the alternate site, and evidently he spent the summer adding second base defense to his portfolio. Given the Reds' depth at second and third, it's not necessarily an indictment that India didn't get time in the bigs in 2020. That said, although the college power is theoretically still in there, the longer it goes without manifesting the more concerned we become.

**Variance:** Medium. He can probably hold down second or third and get on base at a decent clip without any improvement, but the delta on his power output remains significant.

**J.P. Breen's Fantasy Take:** Unless injuries have continued to mask his power potential, there's nothing exciting about India's fantasy profile. He won't run much. He will struggle to hit 20 homers. Plus, he's never hit above .270 as a professional. It all seems … fine. It's just difficult for me to get excited about a dude whose best-case fantasy scenario seems to be Eduardo Escobar, circa 2015-2018.

### 7 Tony Santillan   RHP    OFP: 55   ETA: 2021
Born: 04/15/97   Age: 24   Bats: R   Throws: R   Height: 6'3"   Weight: 240
Origin: Round 2, 2015 Draft (#49 overall)

**The Report:** Have good frame, will travel up the minors. Santillan is the next tier down of mid-rotation types who dot the back of the 101 every year (and he hasn't been that far off the last two list cycles). The fastball backed up a little in 2019 and concern about the secondaries and command projection made the reliever risk loom a little larger.

**Development Track:** Santillan was at the alternate site and in consideration for major league time—even made the playoff taxi squad. The velocity has ticked back up and the change and breaker both looked potentially average-or-better. There's still some unanswered questions on whether the command and stamina are good enough to start across 162 games, but at least there are fewer questions about the stuff now.

**Variance:** Medium. There's some profile risk and Santillan might fit best as a bulk inning guy after an opener. He's trending in the right direction though and should see the majors this season.

**J.P. Breen's Fantasy Take:** We're talking about a potential fourth starter who had injury and performance issues in 2019? That juice ain't worth the squeeze outside of dynasty leagues that roster 200-plus prospects. If Santillan's velocity has returned, as suggested above, he's somewhat more interesting due to his proximity to the big leagues. Still, given that he hasn't struck out more than a batter per inning since 2016 and has a history of command problems, he shouldn't be considered to be anything more than roster backfill.

### 8. Michael Siani  CF    OFP: 50   ETA: 2023/2024
Born: 07/16/99   Age: 21   Bats: L   Throws: L   Height: 6'1"   Weight: 188
Origin: Round 4, 2018 Draft (#109 overall)

**The Report:** Siani continued to get glowing reviews for his center field defense at the alternate site and at instructs, which is consistent with the speed, first step, and throwing arm he had already established as strengths. He won't need to hit too much to be a contributor, but all phases of his offensive game remain raw, and when we last got looks at him, his swing seemed designed for contact over power, which would theoretically take advantage of his plus speed.

**Development Track:** Given the above, Siani losing a summer of at-bats is particularly painful, both for his development and for our sense of how well he is progressing at the plate. He did get a chance to face older competition at the alternate site, even if it wasn't in formal game action. If his 2019 first-half/second-half narrative was that of a cold weather prep bat adjusting to Low-A, there was theoretically a chance he continued to thrive in High-A and maybe challenge for Double-A this year. With the season gone, there will be that much more pressure to add to his offense next year.

**Variance:** High. While it sounds like it wasn't a lost year for Siani, he was still deprived of what he needed most: a high volume of at-bats against advanced competition.

**J.P. Breen's Fantasy Take:** Siani has a profile that can fall through the dynasty cracks. He swiped 45 bases in 2019, which grabs plenty of people's attention, but neither the offensive scouting reports nor the minor-league batting averages have been good. Still, too many dynasty owners discount Siani's defensive abilities. His glove could get him to the big leagues, and at that point, the speed becomes far more attractive. Guys like Leonys Martín, after all, stick around for years. Sure, you say, but Martin is always available on the waiver wire! Yes, which is why Siani is not worth rostering outside of the deepest of fantasy leagues—y'know, the ones that regularly roster guys like Martin in the majors.

### 9 Rece Hinds   SS      OFP: 50   ETA: 2024
Born: 09/05/00   Age: 20   Bats: R   Throws: R   Height: 6'4"   Weight: 215
Origin: Round 2, 2019 Draft (#49 overall)

**The Report:** Hinds is a big, strong prep draftee, has tons of raw power, swings really, really hard, and just turned 20. As you might imagine, there's plenty of swing-and-miss here and all of the attendant concerns that brings about accessing the power in games and reaching base enough to be a regular.

**Development Track:** Hinds evidently used the summer to semi-officially transition over to third base and, ironically, the lack of games meant that much more time for him to try to shore up the defensive deficiencies in his game at the alternate site. We heard good things about third base as a fit, as we already knew he had the arm strength for the position, and evidently his hands and feet were promising enough that he may be able to stick there for a while.

**Variance:** High. He has 10 professional plate appearances and they were in rookie ball.

**J.P. Breen's Fantasy Take:** Hinds is too far away from the big leagues for the move to third base to matter much for dynasty purposes. As for the bat, he has enough raw power to make him worth monitoring, but he's not worth rostering, even in deep dynasty leagues. The questions about his hit tool and his plate discipline are too loud at the moment.

### 10 Lyon Richardson   RHP
Born: 01/18/00   Age: 21   Bats: S   Throws: R   Height: 6'2"   Weight: 192
Origin: Round 2, 2018 Draft (#62 overall)

**The Report:** Richardson is an athletic prep arm with high-effort mechanics who impressed us sufficiently—despite the profile concerns—to make this list last year. Unsurprising for a non-elite prep pitching prospect, Richardson was inconsistent with the quality and command of the non-fastball offerings. So we were not confident he would stay in the rotation. But if he winds up a reliever, there's the material here for a pretty good one.

**Development Track:** Richardson's velocity was up a tick at the alternate site, sitting 93-94 and touching 96-97, and he was reportedly more consistent with his breaking pitch against the most advanced hitters he has ever faced. On the one hand, that's in a very small sample in non-game action, but on the other hand, pitching prospects with far shinier pedigrees than Richardson's had trouble with their mechanics in the extremely weird "season" and Richardson did not. Every step closer he takes to the majors without being converted to relief is a victory.

**Variance:** High. If he doesn't improve the consistency of his secondaries considerably he's a reliever and the fallback options from there involve pitching in other countries.

**J.P. Breen's Fantasy Take:** No, no, don't speak / I know what you're thinkin' / And I don't need your reasons / Don't tell me cuz it hurts

## The Prospects You Meet Outside The Top Ten:

### Interesting Draft Follows

**Christian Roa**   Born: 04/02/99   Age: 22   Bats: R   Throws: R   Height: 6'4"   Weight: 220   Origin: Round 2, 2020 Draft (#48 overall)
A solid, albeit modest performer in his first two years at Texas A&M, Roa saw his draft stock bump coinciding with a tick up in his velocity this year. Witnessed by many upper-tier evaluators in town to see Asa Lacy, the performance was enough to vault Roa into the second round despite a loss in command toward the end of his abbreviated season. It's a four-pitch mix that's at least average across the board, and with some room still left on his 6-foot-4 frame. The question becomes what further gains can be made with his velocity and whether he can harness the command.

**Bryce Bonnin**   Born: 10/11/98   Age: 22   Bats: R   Throws: R   Height: 6'2"   Weight: 190   Origin: Round 3, 2020 Draft (#84 overall)
The Reds' third-round pick has the kind of raw material—a high-spin 95-mph fastball and potential plus slider—that they'd want their current pitching development team working with. He might not be a starter long term, but he will start for now, and it could be a short hop to major league help if and when he moves to the bullpen.

### Prospects to dream on a little

**Michel Triana**   Born: 11/23/99   Age: 21   Bats: L   Throws: R   Height: 6'3"   Weight: 230   Origin: International Free Agent, 2019
Another seven-figure Cuban signee for Cincinnati, the bat here is worth flagging even though he has been playing mostly first base. There's big power potential here, but the hit tool is also more advanced than you might think. He's going to have to hit a lot, obviously, but the early returns are good. Check back after he gets more stateside game time.

### Interesting (2019) Draft Follows

**Ivan Johnson**   2B   Born: 10/11/98   Age: 22   Bats: S   Throws: R   Height: 6'0"   Weight: 190   Origin: Round 4, 2019 Draft (#114 overall)

Last season's low minors sleeper remains buzzy coming off instructs. He might not be a shortstop long term, but for now you can keep dreaming on a switch-hitting shortstop with pop and some feel for hitting. You can also pencil him in as a 2021 breakout candidate even if he has to slide over to second or third.

**Tyler Callihan   2B**   Born: 06/22/00   Age: 21   Bats: L   Throws: R   Height: 6'1"   Weight: 205   Origin: Round 3, 2019 Draft (#85 overall)
Callihan is another of the Reds' bat-first infield prospects who they hope to refine enough to manage at second or third while the bat plays up enough to make it worthwhile. A 2019 prep draftee, Callihan also will suffer from the loss of 2020 development. The left-handed swing is pretty, and there's still room for physical development with a professional conditioning program as he ages into his 20s.

**Safe MLB bat, but less upside than you'd like**

**TJ Friedl   LF**   Born: 08/14/95   Age: 25   Bats: L   Throws: L   Height: 5'10"   Weight: 180   Origin: Undrafted Free Agent, 2016
Hey, did you know that Friedl got the highest bonus ever given to a UDFA because most teams didn't even know he was draft eligible? It's been relegated to a fun fact over the years and now he's a good glove at three outfield spots with enough OBP to make him a useful bench player as soon as 2021.

**Huge Stuff & Huge Risk**

**Jared Solomon   RHP**   Born: 06/10/97   Age: 24   Bats: R   Throws: R   Height: 6'2"   Weight: 200   Origin:
A former 11th-round pick, the Reds added Solomon to their 40-man roster last week, only a few weeks removed from his having Tommy John surgery. The stuff had popped to the high 90s, scraping triple digits, with reports of a hellacious breaking pitch. Sometimes that can be a precursor to injury and, well … there you go. The risk is extreme and we don't know how much stuff he'll retain after his rehab, but the organization clearly believes in the talent and if they're right that's the type of arsenal worth flagging.

## Top Talents 25 and Under (as of 4/1/2021):

1. Nick Senzel, OF
2. Nick Lodolo, LHP
3. Austin Hendrick, OF
4. Hunter Greene, RHP
5. Tyler Stephenson, C
6. Jose Garcia, SS
7. Jonathan India, IF

# Cincinnati Reds 2021

8. Tony Santillan, RHP
9. Mike Siani, OF
10. Rece Hinds, 3B

2016 No. 2-overall pick Nick Senzel is the only young Reds non-prospect to make our list here. The two-time top-10 global prospect still hasn't quite established himself as a good major-league regular yet, mostly through no fault of his own; in 2020, he missed a month with COVID-19 and didn't hit well on his return. We're still in on his long-term potential with the bat, and the longtime infielder seems to have settled in at a surprising position defensively: center field. We'd like to see what he can do over a healthy, full season. Hopefully, that's 2021.

# Part 3: Featured Articles

# Reds All-Time Top 10 Players

by Steven Goldman

## POSITION PLAYERS

**JOHNNY BENCH, C (1967–1983)**
Almost forty years on there's still little argument against Bench as the greatest catcher off all time. No backstop has exceeded his results at bat in a meaningful way. Those few who could make an argument to have had higher defensive peaks weren't comparable hitters. That the Big Red Machine reached the postseason five times without a Hall of Fame pitcher prior to the late arrival of Tom Seaver makes a further argument in favor of aspects of his receiving skills that weren't tracked at that time.

**JOEY VOTTO, 1B (2007–Present)**
Winding down in his late 30s, but that changes nothing about what came before: Seven years of leading the National League in on-base percentage; only Rogers Hornsby, Barry Bonds, Babe Ruth, and Ted Williams had more OBP titles. He's sometimes faulted for not being more of an RBI man, which is like faulting Maury Wills for hitting so few home runs or Harmon Killebrew for his lack of speed. Votto's central skill is so exceptionally valuable, and so rare, that faulting him for hitting "only" .326 (career) with men on should be in the dictionary of phrases under "missing the forest for the trees." Baseball is a game of keep-the-line moving, prolonging the team's times at bat. Few players in history have been better at that than Votto.

**TONY PEREZ, 1B/3B (1964–1976, 1984–1986)**
Part of a final generation of Cuban-born players to come to the United States before hostile relations between the two countries eliminated the possibility for decades, Perez had seven 100-RBI seasons, six of them for the Reds. Quietly a team leader—"He could hand it out rougher than anyone yet somehow he could

do it without offending," manager Sparky Anderson said, Perez had to decide between playing baseball in America and being with his family. As a result, he once went 10 years without seeing his parents. That's leadership.

**PETE ROSE, INF/OF (1963–78, 1984–1986)**
Due to all of the controversy surrounding the end of his career it's easy to forget he was unique, combining an approach that was high-contact, yet selective, with an extraordinarily long peak: From his age-24 season through age-38 he hit .316/.388/.442. Most players don't get 14 years in the majors, never mind 14 great seasons, but Rose left room for bookends.

**JOE MORGAN, 2B (1972–1979)**
A nearly flawless player, Morgan checked all the boxes: Power, patience, batting average, speed, defense, and intelligence. GM Bob Howsam's decision to trade Tommy Helms, Lee May, and Jimmy Stewart to Houston to get Morgan and four other players was among the boldest strokes in the history of team-building given the popularity of the players he was discarding and Morgan's prior record, which included a mix of excellence, production suppressed by injuries and the Astrodome, and conflicts with a manager who was less than enlightened when it came to players of color. "If the United States had traded Dwight Eisenhower to the Germans during World War II," the Cincinnati Enquirer's Bob Hertzel wrote in panning the deal due to its negative effect on the club's leadership quotient on November 30, 1971, "it wouldn't have been much different than sending May and Helms to Houston." Two MVP awards later, it was clear that Howsam and Morgan had more than earned the last laugh.

**HEINIE GROH, 3B (1913–1921)**
Henry Groh was traded from the Giants to the Reds as part of a package for pitcher Art Fromme, one of the best trades in Reds history (or one of the worst of John McGraw's career, depending on your point of view). Famous for his bottle-bat, which helped with bunting and making contact, Groh was also a shockingly sure-handed defensive player for the small-glove, grounder-heavy era in which he played. His career .967 fielding percentage is comparable to that of modern players like Manny Machado, Kyle Seager, and Evan Longoria. As a hitter he twice led the NL in on-base percentage and (after a trade back to the Giants), hit .474 in the 1922 World Series.

**DAVE CONCEPCION, SS (1970–1988)**
Still top-10 all time in games played at short, the five-time Gold Glove-winner was a solid offensive player at his peak, hitting a roughly league-average .282/.334/.389 from 1973 through 1982. In an era of offensive-minded shortstops,

it's easy to forget what robust production that was for a shortstop in the age of Mark Belanger. Concepcion was listed as the Reds' number-three hitter over 500 times during his career.

**BARRY LARKIN, SS (1986–2004)**
The fourth-overall pick of the 1985 draft (after B.J. Surhoff, Will Clark and Bobby Witt, ahead of Barry Bonds), Larkin was so good when he played that it was worth waiting out his all too frequent injuries. An exemplar of the power-speed players who dominated the game before it became ruled by strikeouts and home runs, his mix of skills is very much missed today. Today it's hard to credit that as of his rookie year there was some question as to whether he or Kurt Stillwell was the Reds' shortstop of the future, but it's true.

**FRANK ROBINSON, OF (1956–1965)**
Marvelously self-possessed and yet too often overshadowed by flashier contemporaries, Robinson was one of the greatest right-handed hitters of all time. His numbers were suppressed by the low-scoring era in which he played; today he'd likely be an annual 40-homer man instead of reaching that high just once. During Robinson's 10-year Reds phase he only twice ranked higher than third in a grouping of himself, Willie Mays, and Hank Aaron, and in both seasons he was still behind the Say-Hey Kid. That's a reflection of Robinson's timing, not his skills, and if we add in soft factors like leadership he was second to none.

**VADA PINSON, OF (1958–1968)**
A great power/speed player of the 1960s, through his mid-20s Pinson seemed to be on a Hall of Fame trajectory but his production slacked off after. Through 1965 he had hit .309/.349/.485. After, playing for the Reds and other clubs, he hit .271/.307/.404, which was barely league average. An excellent glove in his younger years, Pinson twice made over 400 putouts in center field; although the feat has been matched as recently as 2017, with the game's present reliance on strikeouts, such accomplishments will increasingly belong to players of the past such as Pinson.

## PITCHERS

**NOODLES HAHN, LHP (1899–1905)**
Frank Hahn—called "Noodles" because as a child he would carry his father's lunchtime soup to him at the piano factory—was a turn-of-the-20th-century control artist who turned pro at the age of 16 due to old-time America's lax standards regarding child labor. In 1901 he went 22-19, one of the few times a pitcher has won 20 games for a team that finished last. Unfortunately, the

375.1 innings he threw that year, part of the heavy workload pitchers typically shouldered at that time (he completed 41 of 42 starts), wore on him and he was out of baseball within a few years.

### BOB EWING, RHP (1902–1909)

"Long Bob" was only 6-foot-1, which goes to show just how short the average American was at the turn of the 20th century. That's not the oddest part of his nickname; his real name wasn't Robert, but George. A spitballer, Ewing had four seasons among the NL leaders in strikeout rate. A longtime semi-pro player, Ewing didn't make it to the majors until he was 29. He peaked with a 1.73 ERA in 1907 but went only 17-19 due to the Reds' subpar attack that year.

### EPPA RIXEY, LHP (1921–1933)

A four-time 20-game winner (and two-time 20-game loser, albeit for the Phillies), Rixey was 6-foot-5 in an era in which the average American was much shorter. With 266 career wins he still ranks 10th all-time among NL pitchers (1900-present). Almost 90 years after he last pitched he still ranks first in career losses with 251. Neither number is reflective of his effectiveness, which allowed to compile a 3.15 ERA over 21 years and a still-massive 4,494.2 innings. Players like Rixey are often dismissed as "compilers," but reliability is a skill.

### DOLF LUQUE, RHP (1918–1929)

One of the earliest star players from Cuba, Luque was a hard thrower who didn't always get offensive support sufficient to give him the gaudy won-lost records he deserved. As a result he was barely over .500 as a Red (154-152) despite consistently posting ERAs that were well below average for the period. The one exception was 1923, when he earned the first of his two ERA titles, 1.93 in 322 innings, and led the NL in wins and winning percentage with a record of 27-8. Among his accomplishments that year: An 11-inning complete game shutout against the Dodgers.

### PAUL DERRINGER, RHP (1933–1941)

A drinking man who threw his fists only slightly less often than he threw pitches, Derringer was a curveballer with a deceptive delivery. He pitched in four World Series, two with the Reds. A four-time 20-game winner, Derringer inadvertently proved the vacuity of individual pitcher won-lost records in 1933 when he went 7-27 in a season split between St. Louis and Cincinnati despite a roughly league-average 3.30 ERA—his offenses averaged two runs of support a game.

### BUCKY WALTERS, RHP (1938–1948)

One of the most famous position-player conversions in history, Walters reached the majors as a third baseman but failed to hit and was shifted to the mound by Phillies manager/ex-catcher Jimmie Wilson. Walters utilized his sinker-slider combination to good but inconsistent results, and it was only after a trade to the Reds, where he was helped by the excellent defense put together by manager Bill McKechnie, that he blossomed into the pitcher who would win the 1939 NL MVP with a record of 27-11 and a league-leading 2.29 ERA. Two more 20-win seasons ensued. It was one of his three seasons in the NL top 10 for strikeout-walk ratio.

**JOE NUXHALL, LHP (1944, 1952–1960, 1962–1966)**
An almost literal baseball lifer who reached the majors at 15 due to wartime manpower shortages and stayed in the game as a broadcaster until 2007, Nuxhall rebounded from his premature, somewhat exploitative promotion to return to the majors and make two All-Star teams. He peaked in 1963 when he struck out 169 and walked just 39 in 217.1 innings.

**JIM MALONEY, RHP (1960–1970)**
A 1960s power-pitcher whose greatness was restricted to his 20s due to arm injuries, Maloney threw two no-hitters, five one-hitters, and left two other no-hitters in progress. A two-time 20-game winner, Maloney once struck out eight Braves in a row, commencing with future Hall of Famer Eddie Mathews—a Hank Aaron groundout ended the streak, at which point Maloney whiffed Matthews again. On June 14, 1965 he struck out 18 Mets in 11 innings but lost the game 1-0. Never received any Cy Young Award consideration because in his two best years Sandy Koufax was a unanimous selection.

**MARIO SOTO, RHP (1977–1988)**
Soto was one of the great pitchers of the 1980s, a cruel decade which tended to see its best hurlers destroyed by injuries before they could pitch long enough to establish their place in history. He threw a mid-to-low 90s fastball and a devastating changeup. This made him exceedingly difficult for same-side hitters, who were held to a .207 career average against him, one of the lowest figures of all time. Unfortunately, he was unable to sustain under an average of 256 innings a year from 1982-through 1985 and was finished at 31.

**JOSE RIJO, RHP (1988–1995, 2001–2002)**
Rushed to the majors by George Steinbrenner in response to Dwight Gooden's popularity, traded to the A's for Rickey Henderson, then dealt to the Reds for the aging Dave Parker before he had turned 23, Rijo finally parlayed his mid-90s fastball and three above-average offspeed pitches into major league dominance. The only downside was frequent arm injuries; the 257.1 innings he threw in 1993 nearly finished him. Still, that season was one of the best by any pitcher of the postwar era. Cy Young voters, overly invested in won-lost records, missed it because he went "only" 14-9. They missed that Rijo had an ERA of 2.86 in his no decisions, 3.52 in losses.

# A Taxonomy of 2020 Abnormalities

## by Rob Mains

I'm going to start this with a trivia question. Trust me, it's relevant. Don't bother skipping to the end of the article to find the answer, it's not there.

*Only five players have appeared in 140 or more games for 16 straight seasons. Who are they?*

It's a trivia question starting off an essay, so you know how this works: Whatever you guessed, you're wrong. It's okay. As someone who purchased this book, chances are good that you're an educated baseball fan. But the circumstances behind 2020 force us to abandon, or at least seriously question, some of our favorite patterns and crutches for evaluating the game we love.

We just completed what was undoubtedly the strangest season in MLB history. No fans, geographically limited schedule, universal DH, seven-inning twin bills, runners on second in extra innings, a 16-team postseason, a club playing at a Triple-A stadium. Some of these changes will likely persist (sorry), but we've never had so many tweaks dumped on us all at once, at least not since they figured out how many balls were in a walk.

And the biggest, of course, was the 60-game season. The 19th century was dotted with teams that went bankrupt before the season ended, but the lone season with only 60 scheduled games was 1877. That year there were only six teams, the league rostered a total of 77 players (just 16 more than the 2020 Marlins), and batters called for pitches to be thrown high or low by the pitcher, who was 50 feet away. We can say the 2020 season was easily the shortest ever for recognizable baseball.

As such, it'll stand out. Few abbreviated seasons do. Just about everybody reading this knows the 1994 season ended after Seattle's Randy Johnson struck out Oakland's Ernie Young for the last out of the Mariners-A's game on August 11. The ensuing player strike wiped out the rest of the season and the postseason. Teams played only 112-117 games that year.

And many of you know that a strike in the middle of the 1981 season split the season in two, resulting in the only Division Series until 1995. Teams played only 103-111 games that year, the shortest regular season since 1885.

Those two seasons are memorable. So when we see that nobody drove in 100 runs in 1981, or that Greg Maddux was the only pitcher with 180 or more innings pitched in 1994, we think, "Of course. Strike year."

But we don't remember other short years. You might not recall that the 1994 strike spilled into the next year, chopping 18 games off the 1995 schedule. You might've read that the 1918 season, played during the last pandemic, ended after Labor Day due to the government's World War I "work or fight" order. A strike erased the first week and a half of the 1972 season, but that year's best known as the last time pitchers batted in the American League.

The point is, while we don't remember small changes to the schedule, we remember the big ones. The 1981 mid-season strike. The 1994 season- and Series-ending strike. And, of course, the pandemic-shortened 2020 season. We won't need a reminder why Marcell Ozuna's 18 homers were the fewest to lead the National League in a century. (Literally; Cy Williams led with 15 in 1920.)

Now, about that trivia question. The five players are Hank Aaron, Brooks Robinson, Pete Rose, Ichiro Suzuki, and Johnny Damon. The one nobody gets, of course, is Damon, and a lot of people miss Ichiro, whose last season of 140-plus games came garbed in the red-orange and ocean blue of Miami when he was 42. That's half of what makes it a good question. The other half is the two guys whom many think made the list but didn't. Lou Gehrig? His streak started in the Yankees' 42nd game of the 1925 season and lasted only 13 seasons after that. And everybody assumes Cal Ripken Jr. did it, having played 2,632 straight games over 17 seasons. But one of those 17 seasons was 1994, when the Orioles played only 112 games.

My point? *I just told you* everybody remembers the 1994 strike year, but everybody forgets it fell in the middle of Ripken's streak, separating the first twelve years from the last four. Just because we recall something doesn't mean it's always at the front of our minds.

Nobody is going to forget 2020, and baseball is obviously not the main reason. But there will come a time in the future when you're looking at a player's or a team's record, and there will be baffling numbers there for 2020, and you'll think, "I wonder what happened." (Not to mention the missing line for minor league players.) Just like you forgot that the 1994 strike limited Ripken to 112 games.

Try not to forget it, though. The 2020 season resulted in weird statistical results for several reasons.

**There were only 60 games.**

I know, duh. But that had impacts beyond counting stats like Ozuna's home run total or Yu Darvish and Shane Bieber leading the majors with eight wins. (I know, pitcher wins, but still.)

The 162-game season is the longest among major North American sports, and that duration gives us a gift. Over the course of a long season, small variations tend to even out. A player who has a ten-game hot streak will probably have a ten-game cold streak. A team that starts the year losing a bunch of close games will probably win a bunch of them. We get regression to the mean. Statistics stabilize.

Consider flipping a coin. Over the long run, we expect it to come up heads about half the time. But the fewer flips, the more variation there'll be. If you flip a coin six times, probability theory tells us you'll get at least two-third heads about 34 percent of the time. Flip it 30 times, your chance of two-thirds heads drops to five percent.

Or, relevant to this case, if you flip a coin 60 times, your chance of getting at least 36 heads—that's 60 percent—is 7.75 percent. Expand the coin-flipping to 162 times, and the chance of getting 60 percent heads drops to 0.73 percent.

In other words, the odds of an outcome that's 20 percent better (or worse) than expected is *more than ten times higher* when you flip your coin 60 times than when you do it 162 times. Call it small sample size, call lack of mean reversion, or call it luck not evening out, 162 is a lot more predictive than 60. You get much more variation over 60 games than over 162. Bieber's 1.63 ERA and 0.87 FIP aren't something we'd see over a full season, and neither is Javier Baéz's .203/.238/.360.

Some players' lines in 2020 look normal. Brian Anderson had an .811 OPS in 2019 and an .810 OPS in 2020. (He probably would have gotten that last point if he'd been given enough time.) But there are many like Bieber and Baéz, some of them from young players still establishing their talent levels. The answer to the question, "What went right or wrong for that guy in 2020?" is most likely "Nothing, it was just a 2020 thing."

**Preseason training was abbreviated for hitters.**
Every year, spring training drags. Players get tired of it, fans get tired of it, and you sure can tell sportswriters get tired of it. Yes, something to get everyone into shape is necessary, but does it really have to drag on for over a month? Can't we shorten it?

The 2020 season answered in the negative, at least for hitters. Warren Spahn is credited with saying that hitting is timing and pitching is upsetting timing. It appears nobody had his timing down after the abbreviated July summer camp. Through August 9—18 games into the season—MLB batters were hitting .230/.311/.395 with a .275 BABIP. That BABIP, had it held, would have been the lowest since 1968, the Year of the Pitcher. In recent years it's hovered around .300.

It didn't hold. Play returned to more normal levels the rest of the year: .249/.325/.425 with a .297 BABIP starting August 10. But batters whose play concentrated in those first two weeks wound up with ugly lines. Andrew

Benintendi went on the injured list with a season-ending rib cage strain on August 11. His final line: .103/.314/.128 in 14 games. Franchy Cordero went on the IL with a hamate bone fracture on August 9 and a .154/.185/.231 line. Even though he came back strong in a late September return, it was too late to repair his full-season numbers.

**Preseason training was abbreviated for pitchers.**

Every year, spring training drags. Players get tired of it, fans get tired of it … wait, I already said that. But the abbreviated preseason was tough on pitchers, too. As noted, they had the upper hand coming out of the gate. But then they lost that hand. And then their arms, too.

The 2020 season was spread over 67 days. During those 67 days, 237 pitchers hit the Injured List, compared to 135 in the first 67 days of 2019. A lot of those IL stints, though, were COVID-19-related. Still, over the first 67 days of the 2019 season, there were 72 pitchers on the IL with arm injuries. That figure jumped to 110 in 2020, a 53 percent increase.

There are a number of factors contributing to pitcher arm injuries, ranging from usage to velocity, but it appears that attenuated preseason training played a role. A lot of pitchers had super-short seasons due to arm woes. Corey Kluber, Roberto Osuna, and Shohei Ohtani combined for seven innings, none after August 8. All suffered arm injuries. We'll never know whether they'd have fared better with a longer preseason, but we can guess how they probably feel.

**Everybody played.**

Rosters were set to expand from 25 to 26 in 2020, so even if we'd had a normal season, we'd have likely seen 2019's record of 1,410 players on MLB rosters broken. But due to the pandemic, rosters started the year at 30 and were cut to only 28. Add multiple COVID-19 absences and the revolving door caused by poor starts by hitters and a rash of pitcher arm injuries, and 1,289 players appeared in MLB games in 2020. The comparable figure over the first 67 days of the 2019 season was 1,109. That 16 percent increase works out to an average of six more players per team in 2020 compared to a similar slice of 2019. A future look back at 2020 rosters will include a lot of unfamiliar names.

**Plus became a minus.**

In advanced metrics, we adjust batter and pitcher performance for park and league/era variations. A plus sign appended to the end of a measure means that it's adjusted for park and league. It's scaled to an average of 100, with higher figures above average and lower figures below average. (Similarly, a metric with a minus is also park- and league-adjusted and scaled to 100, with lower values better.) Here at BP, our advanced measure of offensive performance is DRC+. Baseball-Reference has OPS+ and FanGraphs has wRC+.

Using park and league adjustments, we can compare Dante Bichette's 1995 Steroid Era season at pre-humidor Coors Field (.340/.364/.620, 40 homers, 128 RBI, MVP runner-up) with Jim Wynn's 1968 Year of the Pitcher season at the cavernous Astrodome (.269/.376/.474, 26 homers, 67 RBI, no MVP votes). It's not close. DRC+, OPS+, and wRC+ all give the nod to Wynn, handily. This is a useful tool. As my Baseball Prospectus colleague Patrick Dubuque tweeted last fall, "Please note that when I ask how you are, I am already adjusting for era."

The 2020 season messes up plus (and minus) stats for two reasons. First, the park adjustment was based on only 30 home games instead of the usual 81. Everything noted above regarding the short season applies, literally doubly, to park effect calculations. DRC+ uses a single-season park factor. OPS+ uses a three-year average and wRC+ five years. The figure for 2020 is suspect.

Second, OPS+ and wRC+ adjust for league: American and National. (DRC+ adjusts for opponent, regardless of league.) While there were two leagues in 2020, they were an artificial construct. To reduce travel, teams played opponents geographically, not based on league. There weren't two leagues, American and National. There were three, Western, Central, and Eastern.

That makes a difference because teams in the same league played in different run-scoring environments. AL teams scored 4.58 runs per game, NL teams 4.71. That's a small difference. But teams in the East scored 0.21 more runs per game (4.95) than teams in the West (4.74), and they both scored a lot more than Central teams (4.25). Adjusting for league misses that difference, so this book will be safe in that regard, but other sources may be distorted somewhat.

**Not every game was a "game."**
In 2020, the rising tide of strikeouts was finally stemmed. Strikeouts per team per game fell from 8.8 in 2019 to 8.7 in 2020. That marked the first decline after 14 straight annual increases.

In 2020, the rising tide of strikeouts rose higher. Batters struck out in 23.4 percent of plate appearances compared to 23.0 percent in 2019. That marked the 15th straight annual increase.

Both are true statements.

Because of two rule changes—seven-inning doubleheaders and runners on second in extra innings—games in 2020 were unprecedented in their brevity. There were 37.0 plate appearances per game in 2020. The only years with fewer were 1904 and 1906-1909. The average game in 2020 entailed 8.61 innings pitched, the fewest since 1899.

So when you see any per-game stats for 2020, you need to increase them by 3 or 4 percent to get them on equal footing with recent years.

## Cincinnati Reds 2021

Or, better, just ignore them. Last year happened. There were major league games contested between major league teams. But when you're looking at those physical or electronic baseball cards, when you're weaving narratives over why this young player's inevitable rise to stardom fell apart or why that old veteran rekindled his magic, don't linger on the 2020 line. It was just too weird.

*Thanks to Lucas Apostoleris for research assistance.*

*—Rob Mains is an author of Baseball Prospectus.*

# Tranches of WAR

## by Russell A. Carleton

We ask "replacement level" to be a lot of things. Sometimes contradictory things. Sometimes I wonder if we know what it even means anymore. The original idea was that it represented the level of production that a team could expect to get from "freely available talent", including bench players, minor leaguers, and waiver wire pickups. It created a common benchmark to compare everyone to, and for that reason, it represented an advancement well beyond what was available at the time. In fact, it created a language and a framework for evaluating players that was not just better but *entirely* different than what came before it.

But then we started mumbling in that language. The idea behind "wins above replacement" was one part sci-fi episode and one part mathematical exercise. Imagine that a player had disappeared before the season and suddenly, in an alternate timeline, his team would have had to replace him. The distance between him and that replacement line was his value. We need to talk about that alternate timeline.

Without getting too into 2:00 am "deep conversations" with extensive navel-gazing, it's worth thinking about why one player might not be playing, while another might.

- A player might not be playing because he has a short-term injury or his manager believes that he needs a day off.
- A player might not be playing because he has a longer-term injury that requires him to be on the injured list.

There's a difference here between these two situations. In particular, the first one generally *doesn't* involve a compensatory roster move, while the second one does. It's possible, though not guaranteed, that the person who will be replacing the injured/resting player would be the same in either case. That matters. Teams generally carry a spare part for all eight position players on the diamond, although in the era of a four-player bench, those spare parts usually are the backup plan for more than one spot.

## Cincinnati Reds 2021

A couple of years ago, I posed a hypothetical question. Suppose that a team had two players in its system fighting for a fourth outfielder spot. One of them was a league average hitter, but would be worth 20 runs below average if allowed to play center field for a full season. One of them was a perfectly average fielder, but would be 15 runs below average as a hitter, if allowed to play an entire season. Which of the two should the team roster? It's tempting to say the second one, as overall, he is the better player. That misses the point. A league average hitter on the bench isn't just a potential replacement for an injured outfielder. He might also pinch hit for the light-hitting shortstop in a key spot. You keep the average hitter on the roster, even though he isn't a hand-in-glove fit for one specific place on the field, because being a bench player is a different job description than being a long-term fill-in for someone. If you find yourself in need of a longer-term fill-in, you can bring the other guy up from AAA.

When we're determining the value of an everyday player though, if he had disappeared before the season and a team would have had to replace his production, they likely would have done it with a player who was a long-term fill-in type because they would have had to replace a guy who played everyday. Maybe that's the same guy that they would have rostered on their bench anyway, but we don't know. It gets to the query of what we hope to accomplish with WAR. Are we looking for an accurate modeling of reality or are we looking for a common baseline to compare everyone to? Both have their uses, but they are somewhat different questions.

Let's talk about another dichotomy.

- A player might not be playing because he isn't very good and is a bench-level player.
- A player might not be playing because there is another player on the team who has a situational advantage that makes him the better choice today. The classic case of this is a handedness platoon. On another day, he might be a better choice.

When we think about player usage, I think we're still stuck in the model that there are starters and there are scrubs. We have plenty of words for bench players or reserves or backups or utility guys. We do still have the word "platoon" in our collective vocabulary, but in the age of short benches, it's hard to construct one. It's always been hard to construct them. You have to find two players who hit with different hands, have skill sets that complement each other, and probably play the same position. In the era of the short bench, one of them had probably better double as a utility player in some way. Baseball has a two-tiered language geared toward the idea of regulars and reserves. The fact that it was so easy for me to find plenty of synonyms for "a player whose primary function is to come into a game to replace a regular player if he is injured or resting" should tell you something.

I'm always one to look for "unspoken words" in baseball. What is it called when someone is both half of a platoon and the utility infielder? That guy exists sometimes, but he reveals himself in that role—usually by accident. We don't have a word for that, and whenever I find myself saying "we don't have a word for that", I look for new opportunities. What do you call it, further, when the job of being the utility infielder is decentralized across the whole infield with occasional contributions from the left fielder? It's not even a "super-utility" player. What happens when you build your entire roster around the idea that everyone will be expected to be a triple major?

⚾ ⚾ ⚾

I think someone else beat me to this one, and on a grand scale. Platoons work because we know that hitters of the opposite hand to the pitcher get better results than hitters of the same hand, usually to the tune of about 20 points of OBP. If you want to express that in runs, it usually comes out to somewhere around 10 to 12 runs of linear weights value prorated across 650 PA. But hang on a second, now let's say that we have two players who might start today, both of roughly equal merit with the bat. One has a handedness advantage, but is the worse fielder of the two. In that case, as long as his "over the course of a season" projection as a fielder at whatever position you want to slot him into is less than a 10-run drop from the guy he might replace, then he's a better option today.

We're not used to thinking of utility players as bat-first options, who would play below-average defense at three different infield positions. That guy might hook on as a 2B/3B/LF type (Howie Kendrick, come on down!) but teams usually think to themselves that they need as their utility infielder someone who "can handle" shortstop, the toughest of the infield spots to play. If someone can do that *and* hit well, he's probably already starting somewhere, so he's not available as a utility infielder. It's easier for those glove guys to find a job. In a world where the replacement for a shortstop *has to be* the designated utility infielder, that makes sense.

But as we talked about last week, we're living in a different world. The rate at which a replacement for a regular starter turns out to be *another starter* shifting over to cover has gone way up over the last five years. There was always some of it in the game, but this has been a supernova of switcheroos. Now if your second baseman is capable of playing a decent shortstop, that 2B/3B/LF guy can swap in. He's not actually playing shortstop, and maybe the defense suffers from the switch, but if he's got enough of a bat, he might outhit those extra fielding miscues. And in doing so, he is effectively your backup shortstop.

Somewhere along the lines, teams got hip to the idea of multi-positional play from their regulars. I've written before about how you can't just put a player, however athletic, into a new position and expect much at first. The data tell us that. Eventually, players can learn to be multi-positionalists, but it takes time, roughly on the order of two months, before they're OK. But there's a hidden message in there. If you give a player some reps at a new spot, he's a reasonably gifted athlete and somewhat smart and willing to learn, he could probably pick it up enough to get to "good enough," and it doesn't take forever. You just have to be purposeful about it. Maybe you get to the point where you can start to say "he's still below average but we could move him there and get another bat into the lineup, and it's a net win."

Teams have started to build those extra lessons into their player development program. It used to be seen as a mark of weakness to be relegated to "utility player" because that meant that you were a bench player (all those synonyms above come with a side of stigma). Now, it's a way of building a team. If you get a few reps in the minors (where it doesn't count) at a spot, you'll have at least played the spot at game speed before. There are limits to how far you can push that. A slow-footed "he's out in left field because we don't have the DH" guy is never going to play short, but maybe your third baseman can try second base and not look like a total moose out there.

⚾ ⚾ ⚾

Back to WAR. I'd argue that the world of starters and scrubs is slowly disintegrating, for good cause. In the event that a regular starter really does go down with an injury–ostensibly, the alternate universe scenario that WAR is attempting to model–it makes the team a little more resilient to replacing him. And the good news is that you're more likely to be able to replace him with the best of the bench bunch, rather than the third-best guy, because the best guy doesn't have to be an exact positional match for the guy who got hurt. And that's what the manager would want to do. He'd want to replace that long-term production, not with an amalgam of everyone else who played that position, but with the best guy available from his reserves.

Now this is still WAR. We still want to retain the principle that we should be measuring a player, and not his teammates. We need some sort of common baseline, and despite what I just said, we'll still need some sort of amalgam. To construct that, I give to you the idea of the tranche. The word, if you've not heard it before, refers to a piece of a whole that is somehow segmented off. It's often used in finance to talk about layers of a financial instrument.

Here, I want you to consider that there are 30 starters at each of the seven non-battery positions (catchers should have their own WAR, since only a catcher can replace a catcher). We can identify them by playing time, and we can futz around with the definition a little bit if we need to. Next, among those who aren't in that starting pool, we identify the top tranche of the 30 best bench players, which I would again identify by playing time, and then the second and third and fourth and so on. If a player were to disappear, his manager would probably want to take a guy from that top tranche of the bench to replace him. In a world where even the starters can slide around the field, that becomes more feasible.

We can take a look at that top tranche and say "How many of them showed that they are able to play (first, second, etc.)?" and therefore could have directly substituted for the starter? How many of them could have been a direct substitute for our injured player? We don't know whether one of them would be on *a specific* team, but we can say that 40 percent of the time, a manager would have been able to draw from tranche 1 in filling the role, and 35 percent from tranche 2. But on tranche 1, we can also look at how many of those players played a position that could have then shifted and covered for that spot. We'd need some eligibility criteria for all of this (probably a minimum number of games played) but it would just be a matter of multiplication. Shortstop would be harder to fill, and managers would probably be dipping a little further down in the talent pool, and so replacement level would be lower, as it is now.

Doing some quick analysis, I found that the difference in just batting linear weights (haven't even gotten into running or fielding) between tranche 1 and tranche 2 in 2019 was about 6.5 runs, prorated across 650 PA. Between tranche 1 and tranche 3, it's 10.8 runs. The ability to shift those plate appearances up the ladder has some real value.

This part is important. We can also give credit to starters for the positions that they showed an ability to play, even if they didn't play them (this is the guy fully capable of playing center, but who's in a corner because the team already has a good center fielder) because he allows a team to carry a player who hits like a left fielder to functionally be the team's backup center fielder. He facilitates that movement upward among the tranches. We can start to appreciate the difference between a left fielder who would never be able to hack it in center (and the compensatory move that his team would have to make) and the left fielder who could do it, but just didn't have to very often.

Past that, you can continue to use whatever hitting and fielding and running metrics you like to determine a player's value, but when we get down to constructing that baseline, I'd argue we need a better conceptual and mathematical framework. It's going to require some more #GoryMath than we're used to, but I'd argue it's a better conceptualization of the way that MLB actually plays the game in 2020. If…y'know…MLB plays in 2020. If WAR is going to be our flagship statistic among the *acronymati*, then we need to acknowledge that it contains some old and starting-to-be-out-of-date assumptions about the game. We may need to tinker with it. Here's my idea for how.

—*Russell A. Carleton is an author of Baseball Prospectus.*

# Secondhand Sport

## by Patrick Dubuque

Back before time stopped, I liked to go to thrift stores. Now that I'm older, I rarely ever buy anything—I don't need much in my life, now—but I still enjoy the old familiar circuit: check to see if there are baseball cards to write about, look for board or card games to play with the kids, scan for random ironic jerseys, hit the book section. It takes ten, maybe fifteen minutes. Thrift stores are the antithesis of modern online shopping, because you don't know what they have, and you don't even really know what you want. It's junk, literal junk, stuff other people thought was worthless. That's what makes it great.

In an idealized economy, thrift stores shouldn't exist. Everybody has a living wage, and every product has a durability that exactly matches its desired life; nothing should need to be given away, no one should need to be given to. But then, thrift stores shouldn't work on a customer experience level, either. You wouldn't think an ethos of "let's make everything disorganized and hard to find" would lead to customer satisfaction, but low-budget retailers like TJ Maxx and Ross thrive on this model. People like bargain hunting as much for the hunting as the bargain; it's part of the experience, spending time as if it's a wager. There's a thrill, occasionally, in inefficiency.

In sports, the modern overuse of the word "inefficiency" is a condemnation: It insinuates that there is *an* efficiency, a correct way to be found, and that all other ways are wrong ways. It's prevalent in baseball but hardly contained to it; the lifehack, the Silicon Valley disruption are other examples of productivity creep in our daily lives. Their modern success makes plenty of sense. Maximization of resources, after all, is its own puzzle, and an industry of European board games is founded upon it. It's fun to take a system and optimize it, unravel it like a sudoku puzzle. If there's only one kind of genius, after all, there's no way anyone can fail to appreciate it.

Baseball has been hacking away at these perceived inefficiencies since its inception: platoons, bullpens, farm systems were all installed to extract more out of the tools at hand. But it's been a particular badge of the sabermetric movement, from Ken Phelps and his All-Star Team to Ricardo Rincon and the darlings of *Moneyball*. It's business, but it's also an ethos: the idea that there's treasure among the trash, something we all failed to appreciate until someone brought it to light.

It's the myth that made Sidd Finch so enticing, that fuels so many "best shape" narratives and new pitch promises. We all, athletes and unathletic sportswriters, want to believe that there's genius trapped inside us, and that it's just a matter of puzzling out the combination to unlock it. That our art, our style is the next inefficiency, waiting for our own Billy Beane. It's why we root for underdogs, and why we're excited for the Mike Tauchmans and the Eurubiel Durazos, champions of skin-deep mediocrity.

Except we aren't anymore, really. The days of "Free X" have descended beyond the ring of irony and into obscurity. There are still Xs to be freed, or at least one X, duplicated endlessly: Mike Ford, Luke Voit, Max Muncy. The undervalued one-dimensional slugger demonstrated how the game hasn't quite culturally caught up to its logical extreme. But for those who don't fit the rather spacious mold, times are grimmer. As Rob Arthur revealed several months ago, there's been a marked increase in the number of sub-replacement relievers. It's the outcome of a greater number of teams forced to play out games without the talent to win them, but it's also emblematic of the modern tendency of teams to dispose of their disposable assets, burning through cost-controlled arms the way that man chopped down forests in *The Lorax*. Stuff just isn't built to outlive their original owners anymore.

It's unsurprising, given how well-mined the market for inefficiencies has been of late. The disciples of the early analytics departments, and the disciples of those, have proliferated the league, with only a few backwater holdouts. The league has grown smarter, but every team has learned the same lesson. In fact, the phenomenon creates a peculiar kind of feedback loop: As teams value a specific subset of players or skills, prospective athletes learn to increase their own marketability by conforming themselves to the demands of their prospective employers.

And that's tragic, in the way that the extinction of animals is tragic; a certain amount of biodiversity in baseball has been lost. Shortstops hit like outfielders. Pitchers don't hit at all. Only the catchers remain idiosyncratic, thanks to the defensive demands of their position; eventually they too will be required to produce like everyone else, or they'll meet the fate of their battery mates. A perfect economy requires perfect production.

I mentioned earlier that more and more, I leave thrift stores empty-handed. It is true that I am more discerning than in the past; my bookshelves are full, and there are more streaming films than I will ever be able to watch. But there are other factors at play.

Thrift stores are, in a way, the bond markets of retail. When the economy is rough and other retailers are struggling, more people look secondhand for their products. But as recently as last year, publications were noting a reversal of the trend: Companies like Goodwill and Savers were expanding despite a strong economy. Publications credited a heightened sense of environmentalism and a rejection of cutting-edge fashion as drivers behind the increase, though the more likely answer is the modern American economy hasn't showered its favors equally, particularly among the young.

But it is more than just the economy. Baseball and thrift stores share something else in common, evident in our current conversations about re-starting the sport: They live in the gray area between public service and private enterprise. Thrift stores provide affordable necessities to lower-class citizens, and collectibles and fashion for the middle-class. Because of the success of the latter, prices have gone up across the board. Especially in terms of clothing, the middle-class flight from fashion into vintage has instead carried the aftereffects of fashion, including its costs, into a territory where people just want clothes. But there's another factor in the rise of prices, in the form of the internet.

The Goodwills of the world have grown smarter, too, employing the internet to extract full value from their detritus. Ebay, similarly, has lost much of the charm it had as a new frontier around the turn of the century. Everything has a price point now; even individual taste is no match for the algorithm, because anything rare, no matter how niche its market, is a collectible to someone.

The internet has had the same effect on thrift stores that sabermetrics has had on baseball; its equivalent to OBP was the bar scanner. As detailed in Slate, the rise of second-party stores on eBay and Amazon birthed an entire industry of used-good salespeople, armed with PDAs and scanners, buying books for three dollars to sell online for five. The author, Michael Savitz, reports earning $60,000 by working nearly 80 hours a week; he makes it clear that this is not a vocation of his choosing. It's long hours, with no real creativity or individuality, skimming the cream off of a local establishment and flipping it to someone with a little more money on the other side of the country. And once the vocation exists, the obvious question arises: why wait to put the wares out on the shelves? Why allow value to exist at all?

Nothing is ruined. Thrift stores will continue to sell polo shirts and DVDs, and baseball will continue to exist and make or lose money, depending on who you believe. But as we continue to refine our knowledge, we lose something in the conquest for efficiency, a delight born out of the unknown. The problem isn't the efficiency itself; we can't blame the booksellers, or the people sweeping freeways to collect grams of platinum from damaged catalytic converters. The problem is a system that requires this sort of profit-skimming behavior in order to feed families (or, for corporations, maximize shareholder return).

# Cincinnati Reds 2021

In times like these, with the 2020 season on the brink and the collective bargaining agreement close behind, it can often feel like the current situation is untenable. It can't keep going like this, even if we don't know what to do about it. But as with thrift stores, there's an equally irresistible feeling that it *has* to keep going, that it would be unimaginable to not have this broken, amazing sport. Both industries exist on an invisible foundation of friction, of chaos and unpredictability, even as both see their foundations buffed down to a perfect, untouchable polish. But if COVID-19 and its financial ramifications do, as some have suggested, make it such that the baseball that returns is fundamentally different than the baseball that came before, perhaps this is the time to lean in, and change the game even more. Fix bunting. Make defense more difficult. Create viable, alternate strategies. Add some chaos back into baseball. It's fun when no one knows quite where things are.

—*Patrick Dubuque is an author of Baseball Prospectus.*

# Steve Dalkowski Dreaming

## by Steven Goldman

We dream of being a pitcher, of starring in the major leagues. Depending on your age and your sense of historical perspective, you might imagine yourself as Walter Johnson, throwing harder than anyone else—hitting more batters than anyone else, too, but always feeling bad about it. You could picture yourself as a Tom Seaver or a David Cone, with all the stuff in the world but still being cerebral about it, thinking about so much more than burning 'em in there. There are so many models one could choose: You could be a Lefty Gomez, Jim Bouton, or Bill Lee, skilled, but not taking the whole thing too seriously, or a Lefty Grove, Bob Gibson, or Steve Carlton, powerful but treating each start like a mission to be survived instead of a game to be enjoyed.

Very few would dream of being Steve Dalkowski, the former Baltimore Orioles prospect who died of COVID-19 last week at the age of 80. Yet, there is something just as noble in Dalkowski's negative accomplishments—and accomplishments is what they are—as there is in the precision-engineered pitching of a Greg Maddux. You have to be very good to be that bad. Dalkowski had all of the stuff of the greatest pitchers but none of the command; his story is not one of failing to conquer his limitations, but striving against one of the cruelest hands that fate or genetics or personality can deal us: A desire to achieve great things which is almost but not quite matched by the ability to meet that goal.

As with Johnson, Grove, Bob Feller, and the rest of the hard-throwing pitchers who played before the advent of modern radar guns, we have to take the word of the players and coaches who saw Dalkowski pitch as to his velocity. He was a hard-drinking, maximum-effort pitcher who, if their memories are to be believed, consistently threw over 100 miles per hour. His was the Maltese Fastball, the stuff that dreams are made of. The problem is that velocity without command and control is still a good distance from utility. Dalkowski was the most effective towel you could design for a fish, the sleekest bathing suit intended to be worn by an astronaut, but that doesn't mean he wasn't beautiful: We can appreciate a journey even if it doesn't end at the intended destination.

Whether because of sloppy mechanics he couldn't calm, an inability to understand that a consistent 98 in the strike zone would likely be more effective than a consistent 110 out of it, or all that beer, Dalkowski could never make the adjustments that pitchers like Feller and Nolan Ryan made before him, possibly because he had so far to go: Feller, who never pitched in the minors, came up at 17 and spent three years walking almost seven batters per nine innings before settling in at 3.8 beginning when he was 20. Ryan started out walking over six batters per nine but gradually improved as his long career played out; for him to go from 6.2 walks per nine with the 1966 Greenville Mets to 3.7 with the 1989 Texas Rangers represents a 40 percent reduction. An equivalent improvement by Dalkowski would still have left him walking over 11 batters per nine innings.

Dalkowski was like *The Room* of pitchers, a player so bad he became good again. Cal Ripken, Sr., who both played with and managed Dalkowski, recalled in a 1979 *Sporting News* "where are they now" piece the occasion when the pitcher crossed up his catcher and his fastball, "hit the plate umpire smack in the mask. The mask broke all to pieces and the umpire wound up in the hospital for three days with a concussion. If they ever had a radar gun in those days, I'll bet Dalkowski would have been timed at 110 miles an hour."

Signed by the Orioles out of New Britain High in Connecticut in 1957, Dalkowski was sent to Kingsport in the Appalachian League, where he pitched 62 innings. He allowed only 22 hits in 62 innings, or 3.2 per nine, a number with no equivalent in major league history (though Aroldis Chapman came close in 2014), and also struck out 121 (17.6 per nine) and walked 129 (18.7). He was also charged with 39 wild pitches. That June, one of his fastballs clipped a Dodgers prospect named Bob Beavers and carried away part of his ear. "The first pitch was over the backstop, the second pitch was called a strike, I didn't think it was," Beavers said last year. "The third pitch hit me and knocked me out, so I don't remember much after that. I couldn't get in the sun for a while, and I never did play baseball again." Former minor leaguer Ron Shelton based the *Bull Durham* pitcher Nuke LaLoosh on Dalkowski. And yet, to see him as a figure of fun, an amusing loser, is to misunderstand something unique and strange.

Dalkowski kept on posting some of the strangest lines in baseball history. Pitching for the Stockton Ports of the Class C California League in 1960, he struck out 262 and walked 262 in 170 innings. Yet, he did improve, especially after pitching for Earl Weaver at Elmira in 1962. Weaver had previously had Dalkowski at Aberdeen in 1959, but wasn't ready to grapple with him then. This time he was. "I had grown more and more concerned about players with great physical abilities who could not learn to correct certain basic deficiencies no matter how much you instructed or drilled them," he related in his autobiography, *It's What You Learn After You Know It All That Counts*. He got permission from the Orioles to give all of his players the Stanford-Binet IQ test. "Dalkowski finished in the 1 percentile in his ability to understand facts. Steve, it was said to say, had the ability to do everything but learn." [sic]

IQ tests are problematic diagnostic tools, so take Weaver's estimate of Dalkowski's mental capabilities with a grain of salt. What's important is that even if he got to the right answer by way of the wrong reason, Weaver had learned something valuable. His insight was to stop asking Dalkowski to learn new pitches and just let him get by with the two that he had. Were Dalkowski a prospect today, that would have been a no-brainer: Can't develop a third pitch? The bullpen is right over there, sir. Player development wasn't like that then, but Weaver, temporarily Dalkowski's mentor, could let him work with what he had. According to Weaver, the pitcher responded: "In the final 57 innings he pitched that season Dalkowski gave up 1 earned run, struck out 110 batters, and walked only 11." It's not true—as per the *Elmira Star-Gazette*, as of late July, Dalkowski had walked 71 in 106 innings and finished with 114 in 160 innings, which means Dalkowski's control actually faded at the end of the season rather than improved—but that doesn't mean it didn't happen in some sense, just that it didn't happen that way. Again, it's the journey, not the destination, and his ERA was 3.04 so *something* had gone right.

Also along the way: The next spring, Orioles manager Billy Hitchcock was rooting for Dalkowski to make the team as a long-man—maybe Weaver had gotten through to him. There were things out of Weaver's control, like the universe's twisted sense of humor: that March, Dalkowski's elbow went "twang."

You sometimes read that it was the Orioles' insistence on Dalkowski learning the curve that did him in, but even if they hadn't learned their lesson, the injury was probably just a coincidence: Dalkowski had thrown an incredible number of pitches over the previous few years. Still, it testifies to the dangers of trying to get what you want and risking the loss of what you had. Dalkowski tried to come back, but the 110-mph stuff was gone. A pitcher with no control and no stuff is…a civilian. What followed were years of vagabond living, arrests for drunkenness. There were Alcoholics Anonymous meetings, assistance from baseball alumni associations, but none of it took. From the 1990s until the time of his passing he dwelt in an assisted living facility, suffering from alcohol-related dementia. He'd been a heavy drinker since his teenage years. As with all those pitches per game, there was a price to be paid. You make choices on the journey and some of them are irrevocable. It's like a fairy tale: "Bite of poison apple? Don't mind if I do."

In the aforementioned *Sporting News* profile, Chuck Stevens, the head of the Association of Professional Ballplayers of America, a ballplayer charity, said, "I've got nothing against drinking. I do it myself sometimes. But, I don't condone common drunkenness. We went through lots of heartache and many dollars, but Dalkowski didn't want to help himself and we weren't going to keep him drunk." The journey is *un*like a fairy tale: No one will come along and kiss it better, not if they're busy forming judgments.

In the end, we are left with a sort of philosophical chicken/egg conundrum: Is failing to meet your goals evidence of unfulfilled potential or the lack of it? Isn't what you did by definition what you were capable of doing? Or could you have broken through to something better with the right help, the right lucky break? These are unanswerable questions, and how we try to answer them may say more about us than about the people we're judging.

No pitcher ever has it easy. *All* pitchers must work hard. *All* pitchers must refine their craft. It's almost never just about *stuff*. Dalkowski dreaming is no insult to the great pitchers who made it; from Pete Alexander to Max Scherzer, they have all earned their way up. And yet, if it is true that we can only do as much as we can do, then the journey would be more of an adventure, the ultimate triumph or defeat more noble, if like Dalkowski we lacked 100 percent of the confidence, the command, the self-possession, the commitment, the resistance to making bad decisions that so many great players possess—to be gloriously human. Or, to put it more succinctly, it would be fun to be able to throw as hard as any person ever has. Even if just for a moment, and even if nothing more came of it than that, no one could say you hadn't lived life to the fullest.

—*Steven Goldman is an author of Baseball Prospectus.*

# A Reward For A Functioning Society

by Cory Frontin and Craig Goldstein

On July 5, Nationals reliever Sean Doolittle said in the middle of a press conference regarding the restart of Major League Baseball and what would later be known as summer camp, "sports are like the reward of a functioning society." This sentence was amidst a much longer, thoughtful reply about the societal and health conditions under which MLB players were being brought back. It's a very similar sentiment to one Jane McManus used on April 7, when she discussed the White House's meeting with sports commissioners. She said "sports are the effect of a functioning society—not the precursor."

Both versions of the same sentiment spoke to a laudable ideal in the context of a country that was not addressing a rampaging virus, and opting instead to bring sports back for the feeling of normalcy rather than the reality of it. "Priorities," as McManus said.

On Wednesday, the NBA's Milwaukee Bucks conducted a wildcat/political strike, refusing to come out for Game 5 of their playoff series against the Orlando Magic. The Magic refused to accept the forfeit, and shortly thereafter other playoff series were threatened by player strikes. Eventually the league moved to postpone that day's games, folding to players leveraging their united power.

The backdrop against which these actions took place was the shooting by police of Jacob Blake. Blake was shot in the back seven times by police, as he attempted to get into his vehicle. He managed to survive the assault, but is paralyzed from the waist down.

⚾ ⚾ ⚾

The step taken to walk out, first by the Milwaukee Bucks, then subsequently by other NBA, WNBA, and MLB teams, was a step toward upholding the virtue of the sentiment described by McManus and Doolittle. But that sentiment does not align with the broad history of sports in this and other countries, a history that contradicts the core of the idealistic statement.

Sports have been a significant part of American society for most of its existence, expanding in importance and influence in recent years. The idea that society was functioning in a way that was worthy of the reward of sports for most of that time is laughable. Much of America is not functioning and has not functioned for Black people, full stop. The oppressed people at the center of this political act by players, specifically Black players, in concert throughout the NBA and in fits and starts throughout Major League Baseball, have not known a society that functions for them rather than *because* of them.

Politics has been part of the sports landscape since the inception of sport, but for just about as long people have bemoaned its presence. Sports are to be an escape, it is said. An escape from what, though? A functioning society?

No, the presence of sports has never signified a cultural or political system that is on the up and up. Rather, the presence of sports *reflect and reinforce the society* that produces them.

⚾   ⚾   ⚾

The Negro Leagues were born out of societal dysfunction. The need for entirely separate leagues, composed of Black and Latino players barred from the Major Leagues because of racism? That is not a functioning society, and yet there were sports.

Even the integration of players from the Negro Leagues resulted in a transfer of power and wealth from Black-owned businesses and communities and into white ones, mirroring the dysfunction that had bled into every aspect of American society at the time. Japheth Knopp noted in the Spring 2016 Baseball Research Journal:

> *The manner in which integration in baseball—and in American businesses generally—occurred was not the only model which was possible. It was likely not even the best approach available, but rather served the needs of those in already privileged positions who were able to control not only the manner in which desegregation occurred, but the public perception of it as well in order to exploit the situation for financial gain. Indeed, the very word integration may not be the most applicable in this context because what actually transpired was not so much the fair and equitable combination of two subcultures into one equal and more homogenous group, but rather the reluctant allowance—under certain preconditions—for African Americans to be assimilated into white society.*

To understand the value of a movement, though, is not to understand how it is co-opted by ownership, but to know the people it brings together and what they demand. When Jackie Robinson—the player who demarcated the inevitability of the end of the Negro leagues—attended the March on Washington for Jobs and Freedom in 1963, he did so with his family and marched alongside the people. He stood alongside hundreds of thousands to fight for their common civil and labor rights. "The moral arc of the universe is long," many freedom fighters have echoed, "but it bends towards justice." The bend, it is less frequently said, happens when a great mass of people place the moral arc of the universe on their knee and apply force, as Jackie, his family, and thousands of others did that day.

⚾   ⚾   ⚾

Of course, taking the moral arc of the universe down from the mantle and bending it is not without risk. Perhaps the outsized influence of athletes is itself a mark of a dysfunctional society, but, nonetheless, hundreds of athletes woke up on Wednesday morning with the power to bring in millions of dollars in revenues. That very power, as we would come to find out, was matched with the equal and opposite power to *not* bring those revenues. That power, in hands ranging from the Milwaukee Bucks, to Kenny Smith in the Inside the NBA Studio, from the unexpected ally, Josh Hader, and his largely white teammates to the notably Black Seattle Mariners, would be exercised for a single demand: the end to state violence against Black people. Not unlike the March itself, it sat at the intersection of the civil rights of Black Americans and bold labor action. The March on Washington stood in the face of a false notion of integration—against an integration of extraction but not one of equality—and proposed something different. Just the same, the acts of solidarity of August 26, 2020 will be remembered in stark defiance of MLB's BLM-branded, but ultimately empty displays on opening weekend.

Bold defiance like this can never be without risk. By choosing to exercise this power, the Milwaukee Bucks took a risk. They risked vitriol and backlash from those they disagreed with. They risked fines or seeing their contracts voided, as a walkout like this is prohibited by their CBA. They risked forfeiting a playoff game, one that, as the No. 1 seed in the playoffs, they'd worked all year to attain. They didn't know how Orlando would respond. It wasn't clear that other teams throughout the league would follow suit in solidarity. And it wasn't known the league would accept these actions and moderately co-opt them by "postponing" games that would have featured no players.

If the league reschedules the games, some of the athletes' risk—their shared sacrifice—will be diminished, in retrospect. But they did not know any of that when they took that risk. And it is often left to athletes to take these risks when others in society won't, especially those of their same socioeconomic status and levels of influence.

It is athletes, specifically BIPOC athletes, that take them, though, because they live with the risk of being something other than white in this country every day. They are no strangers to the realities of police brutality. It seems incongruous then, to say that sports are a reward for a functioning society when we rely on athletes to lead us closer to being a functioning society. Luckily, our beloved athletes, WNBA players first and foremost among them, understand what sports truly are: a pipebender for the moral arc of the universe.

> —*Craig Goldstein is editor in chief of Baseball Prospectus. Cory Frontin is an author of Baseball Prospectus.*

# Index of Names

Akiyama, Shogo ............... 16
Antone, Tejay .................... 38
Aquino, Aristides ............... 18
Bailey, Brandon ................. 81
Balentien, Wladimir ............ 70
Barnhart, Tucker ................ 71
Bedrosian, Cam ................. 40
Biddle, Jesse ..................... 82
Blandino, Alex ................... 72
Bonnin, Bryce .................... 96
Callihan, Tyler .............. 72, 97
Castellanos, Nick ............... 20
Castillo, Luis ..................... 42
Davidson, Matt .................. 73
De León, José .................... 44
Doolittle, Sean ................... 46
Farmer, Kyle ..................... 22
Friedl, TJ .......................... 97
García, Edgar .................... 83
Garcia, Jose ................. 24, 92
Garrett, Amir .................... 48
Gray, Sonny ...................... 50
Greene, Hunter ............. 84, 90
Heineman, Scott ................ 26
Hendrick, Austin ........... 73, 90
Hendrix, Ryan ................... 84
Hinds, Rece ................. 74, 95
Hoffman, Jeff .................... 52
India, Jonathan ............ 74, 93
Jankowski, Travis ............... 75
Johnson, Ivan ................... 96
Kuhnel, Joel ..................... 85
Lodolo, Nick ................ 86, 89
Lorenzen, Michael .............. 54
Mahle, Tyler ..................... 56
Miley, Wade ..................... 58
Moustakas, Mike ................ 28
Osich, Josh ...................... 60
Payton, Mark .................... 76
Pérez, Cionel .................... 62
Ramirez, Noé .................... 64
Richardson, Lyon ............... 95
Rivas, Leonardo ................. 76
Roa, Christian ................... 96
Santillan, Tony ............ 86, 93
Schrock, Max .................... 77
Senzel, Nick ..................... 30
Siani, Michael .............. 77, 94
Sims, Lucas ...................... 66
Smith, Dwight ................... 78
Solomon, Jared ................. 97
Stephenson, Tyler ........ 78, 91
Strange-Gordon, Dee .......... 80
Suárez, Eugenio ................ 32
Thornburg, Tyler ................ 68
Triana, Michel ................... 96
Votto, Joey ...................... 34
Winker, Jesse ................... 36

# For the Joy of Keeping Score

THIRTY81 Project is an ongoing graphic design project focused on the ballparks of baseball. Since being established in 2013, scorecards have been a fundemantal part of the effort. Each two-page card is uniquely ballpark-centric — there are 30 variants — and designed with both beginning and veteran scorekeepers in mind. Evolving over the years with suggestions from fans, broadcasters, and official scorers, the sheets are freely available to everyone as printable letter-size PDFs at the project webshop: www.THIRTY81Project.com

Download, Print, Score, Repeat ...

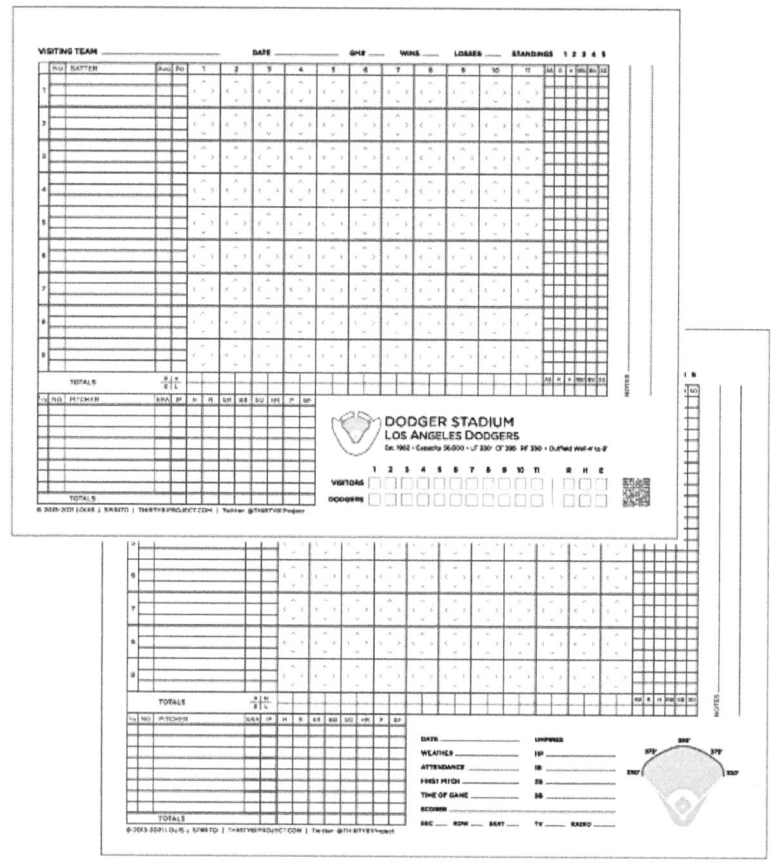

Scorecard design ©2013-2021 Louis J. Spirito | THIRTY81Project